百年典藏

——东华大学图书馆馆藏精品集

东华大学图书馆　编

東華大學 出版社
·上海·

图书在版编目（CIP）数据

百年典藏：东华大学图书馆馆藏精品集/陈惠兰主编.
—上海：东华大学出版社，2017.1
ISBN 978-7-5669-1180-3

Ⅰ.①百… Ⅱ.①陈… Ⅲ.①院校图书馆—图书馆目录—上海—1881-1949 Ⅳ.①Z822.6

中国版本图书馆CIP数据核字（2016）第303348号

责任编辑 吴川灵

百年典藏
——东华大学图书馆馆藏精品集
东华大学图书馆 编
陈惠兰 主编

出　　版：东华大学出版社(上海市延安西路1882号，200051)
本社网址：http://www.dhupress.net
天猫旗舰店：http://dhdx.tmall.com
营销中心：021-62193056 62373056 62379558
电子邮箱：805744969@qq.com
印　　刷：上海龙腾印务有限公司
开　　本：787mm×1092mm 1/16
印　　张：5
字　　数：160千字
版　　次：2017年1月第1版
印　　次：2017年1月第1次印刷
书　　号：ISBN 978-7-5669-1180-3
定　　价：58.00元

序 言

东华大学目前藏有民国纺织书刊千余种，全面记录和展示了中国近代纺织工程与教育的理论与实践，这其中包括一定孤本数量民国纺织图书。为了进一步提升东华大学图书馆的服务水平，使更多的读者感受到我国民国纺织工程理论、实践、教育的特点，策划《百年典藏——东华大学图书馆馆藏精品集》的编写与出版。本书选择具有代表性的书刊100余册，以蚕丝纺织书籍、棉纺织书籍等10个主题分类呈现。这100余册书刊，是纺织记忆中民国纺织书刊的缩影，书刊上留存的图书馆印章从一个侧面述说着民国纺织教育的历史，而书刊上呈现的广告则体现了当年纺织业的繁荣。

历史是最好老师，给每一个国家未来的发展提供启示。本书是我国民国纺织理论和教育历史的索引，可以帮助读者快速寻找民国纺织技术和教育的足迹。图书馆的责任是文献保障和利用，本书编撰的初衷是更好的展示和利用纺织特色珍贵文献，使沉寂在书架上的故纸闪耀文化的光辉，促进更多的人热切关心东华图书馆的特色馆藏建设和利用，并谨以此书感谢社会各界对东华大学图书馆发展的支持。

东华大学图书馆馆长

2016年9月

本书编委会

主　编：陈惠兰

副主编：刘建平

编　委：

陈惠兰

刘建平

吴川灵

高佩音

戴郊步

目 录

索 引

蚕桑织务纪要

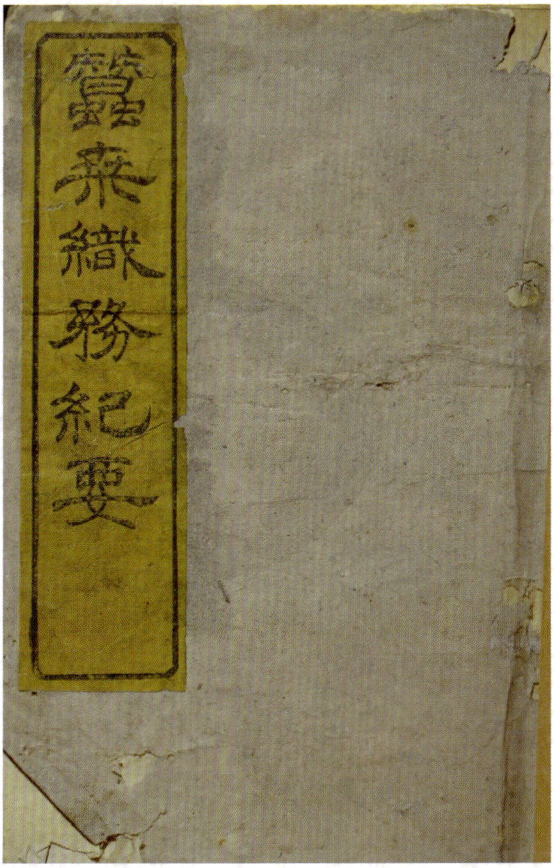

著者：河南蚕桑织务局

出版时间：1881 年，宣纸线装

历史馆藏：南通学院

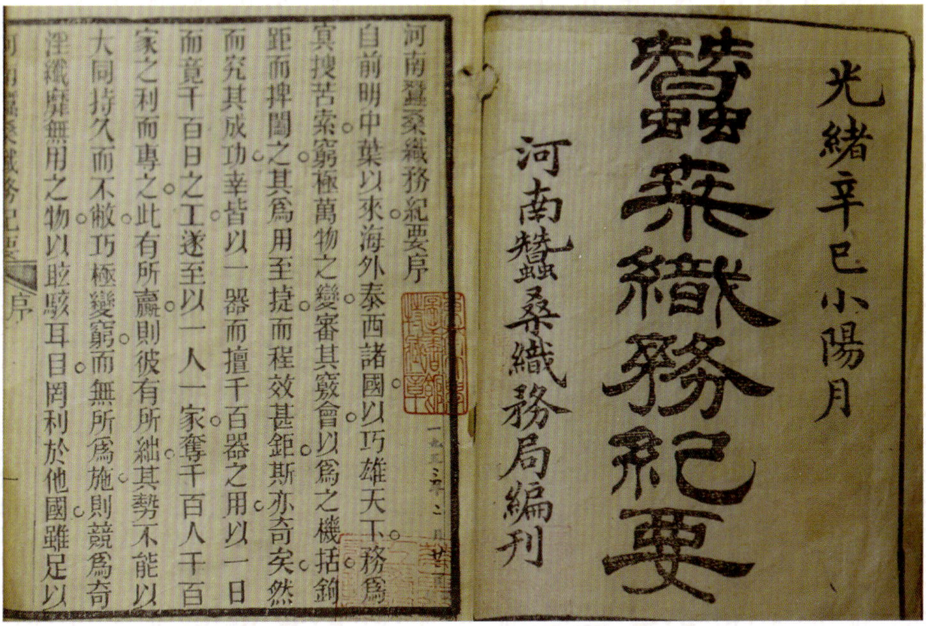

光緒辛巳小陽月

蠶桑織務紀要

河南蠶桑織務局編刊

河南蠶桑織務紀要序

自前明中葉以來海外泰西諸國以巧雄天下務爲冥搜苦索窮極萬物之變審其竅會以爲之機括鉤距而捭闔之其爲用至捷而程效甚鉅斯亦奇矣然而究其成功率皆以一器而擅千百器之用以一日而竟千百日之工遂至以一人一家奪千百人千百家之利而專之此有所贏則彼有所絀其勢不能以大同持久而不敝巧極變窮而無所爲施則競爲奇淫纖靡無用之物以眩駭耳目罔利於他國雖足以

河南蠶桑織務紀要　序　一

制丝新论

著者：赖昌
出版者：上海新学会社
出版时间：1912 年
历史馆藏：南通学院

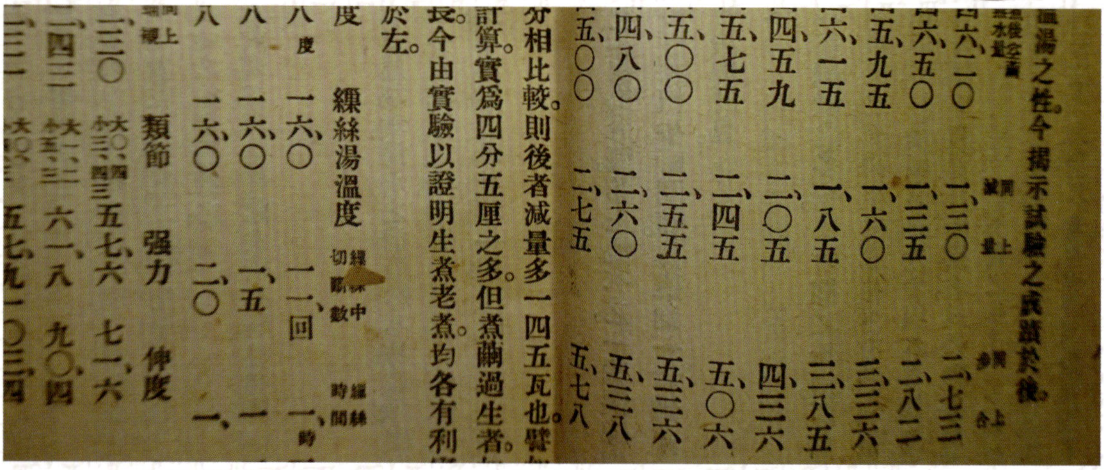

蚕业系列书籍

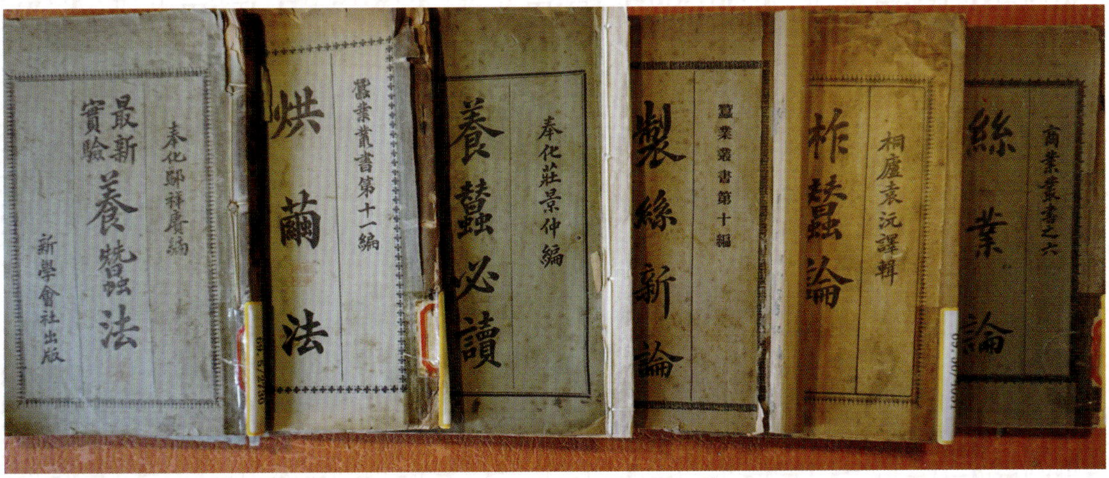

出版者：上海新学会社
出版时间：1912-1923 年
历史馆藏：南通学院

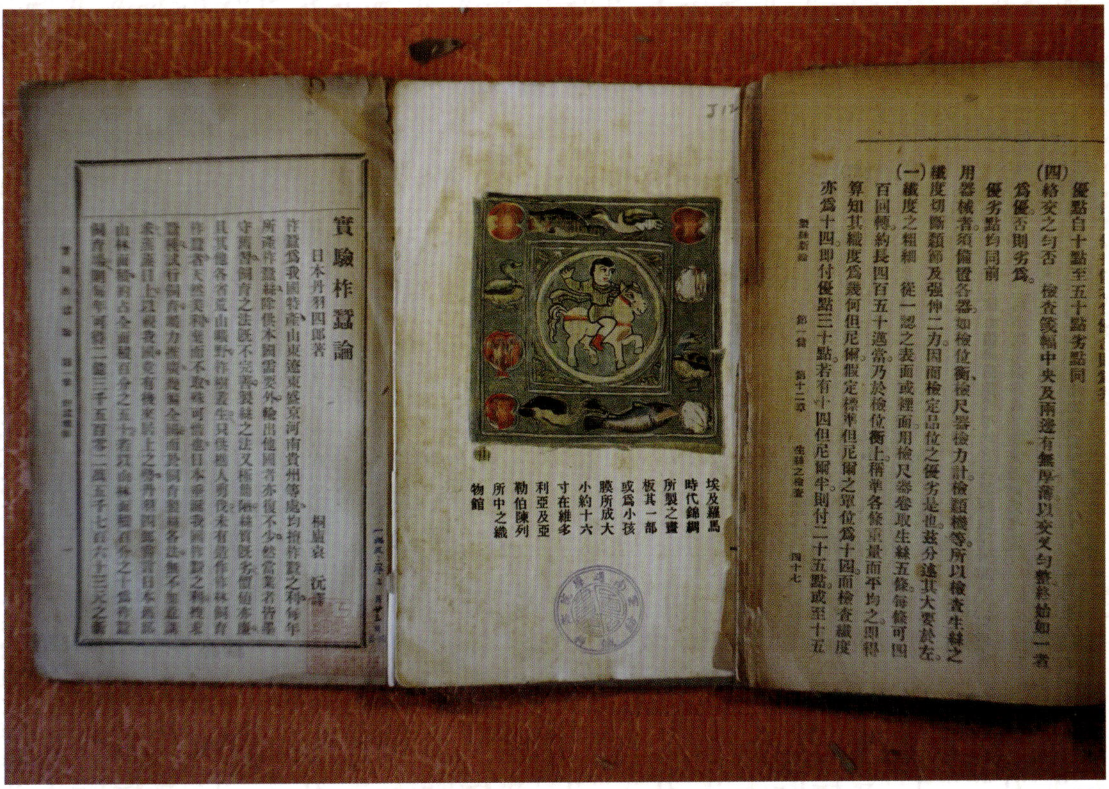

制丝学

著者：三谷彻
出版者：东京明文堂
出版时间：1918 年
历史馆藏：南通学院

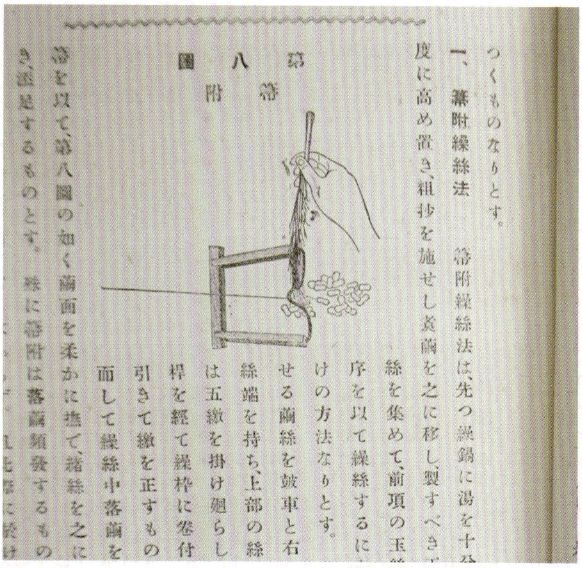

つくものなりとす。
一、箒附繰絲法　箒附繰絲法は、先つ繰鍋に湯を十分
度に高め置き、粗抄を施せし煮繭を之に移し製すべき
絲を集めて、前項の玉
序を以て繰絲するに
けの方法なりとす。
せる繭絲を皷車と右
絲端を持ち、上部の絲
は五繳を掛け廻らし
桿を經て繰枠に卷付
引きて繳を正すもの
而して繰絲中落繭を
箒を以て、第八圖の如く繭面を柔かに撫て、緒絲を之に
き、添足するものとす。　殊に箒附は落繭頻發するもの

第八圖
箒附

Silk

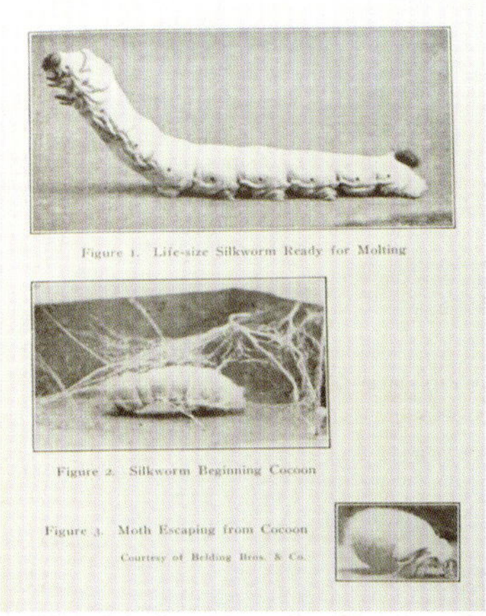

著者：THOMPSON
出版者：NEW YORK THE RONALD PRESS COMPANY
出版时间：1922 年
历史馆藏：南通学院

制丝详说

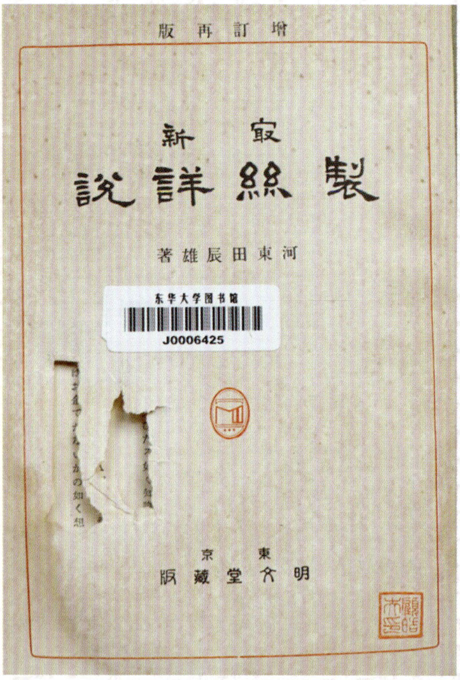

著者：田晨雄
出版者：东京明文堂
出版时间：1926 年

实验生丝整理法

著者：妹尾新藏
出版者：东京明文堂
出版时间：1926 年

Silk Processes Winding, Warping and Quilling

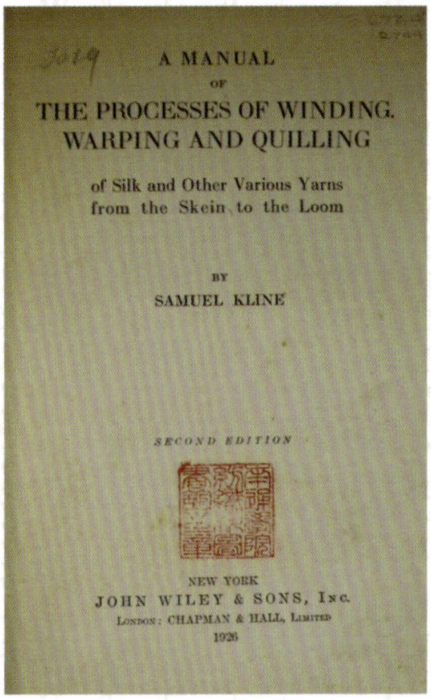

著者：Samuel Kline
出版者：John Wilely & Sons, Inc.
出版时间：1926 年
历史馆藏：南通学院

组合制丝经营策

著者：细川幸重
出版者：东京明文堂
出版时间：1927 年
历史馆藏：南通学院

Second Report of the Raw Silk Classification Committee

出版者：The Silk Association of America Inc.
出版时间：1927 年
历史馆藏：南通学院

The Raw Silk Industry of Japan

编者：Charles J. Huber
出版者：THE SILK ASSOCIATION OF AMERICA, Inc.
出版时间：1929 年
历史馆藏：南通学院

A Raw Silk Classification with Methods of Testing

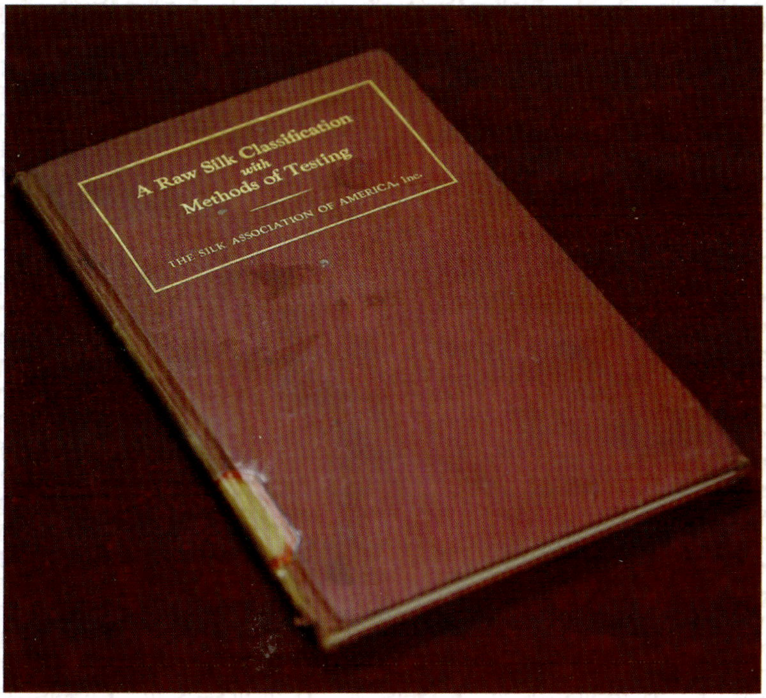

著者：RAMSAYPEUGNET
出版者 :THE SILK ASSOCIATION OF AMERICA, Inc.
出版时间：1929 年
历史馆藏：南通学院

绢纺织学

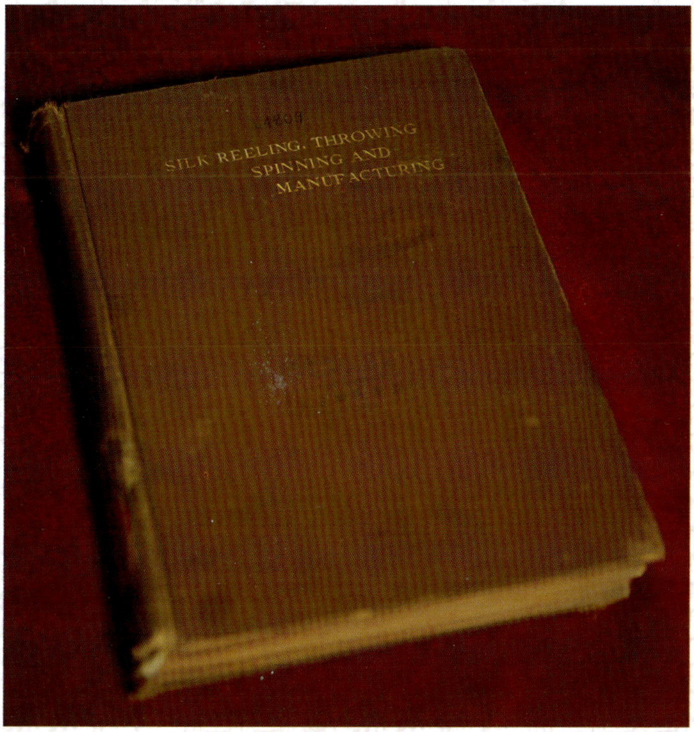

04809
東京高等工業學校教授 大住吾八著
絹 紡 織 學
Silk Reeling, Throwing
Spinning and Manufacturing
—1929—
東 京
丸善株式會社

著者：大住吾八
出版者：东京丸善株式会社
出版时间：1929 年
历史馆藏：南通学院、国立浙江大学、上海财经学院

Raw Silk and Throwing

著者：WARREN.P.SEEM
出版者：McGRAW-HILL BOOK COMPANY, Inc.
出版时间：1929 年
历史馆藏：南通学院

Davison's Silk and Rayon Yarns

出版者：DAVISON PUBLISHING CO.
出版时间：1934 年
历史馆藏：南通学院

Some Difficulties in Cotton Spinning

著者：SIR B. A. DOBSON, C.B., M.I.M.E
出版者：JOHN HEYWOOD
出版时间：1893 年
历史馆藏：青島守备军民政部、青岛工学院

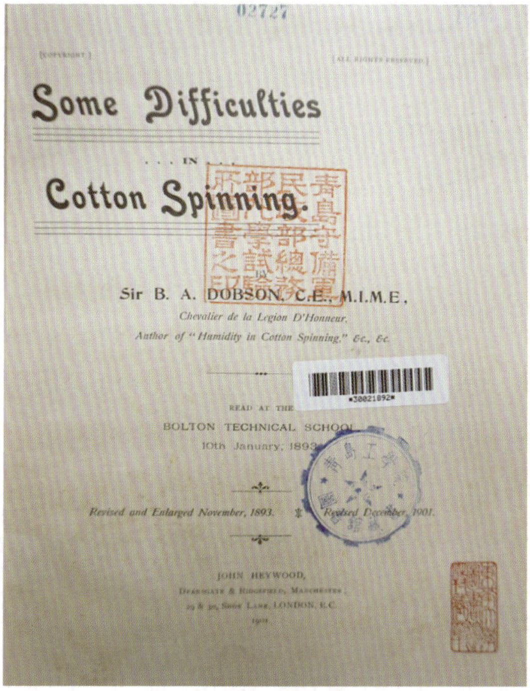
02727

[ALL RIGHTS RESERVED.]

Some Difficulties

. . . IN . . .

Cotton Spinning.

BY

Sir B. A. DOBSON, C.E., M.I.M.E.,

Chevalier de la Legion D'Honneur.

Author of "Humidity in Cotton Spinning," &c., &c.

READ AT THE

BOLTON TECHNICAL SCHOOL

10th January, 1893.

Revised and Enlarged November, 1893. *Revised December, 1901.*

JOHN HEYWOOD,

DEANSGATE & RIDGEFIELD, MANCHESTER;

29 & 30, SHOE LANE, LONDON, E.C.

1901.

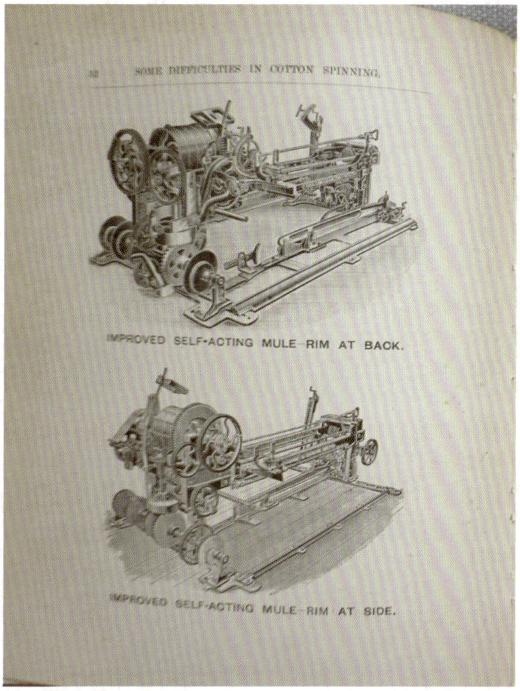

Cotton Spinning

著者：THOMAS THORNLEY
出版者：LONDON SCOTT,GREENWOOD & SON
出版时间：1907 年
历史馆藏：青岛守备军民政部、青岛工学院

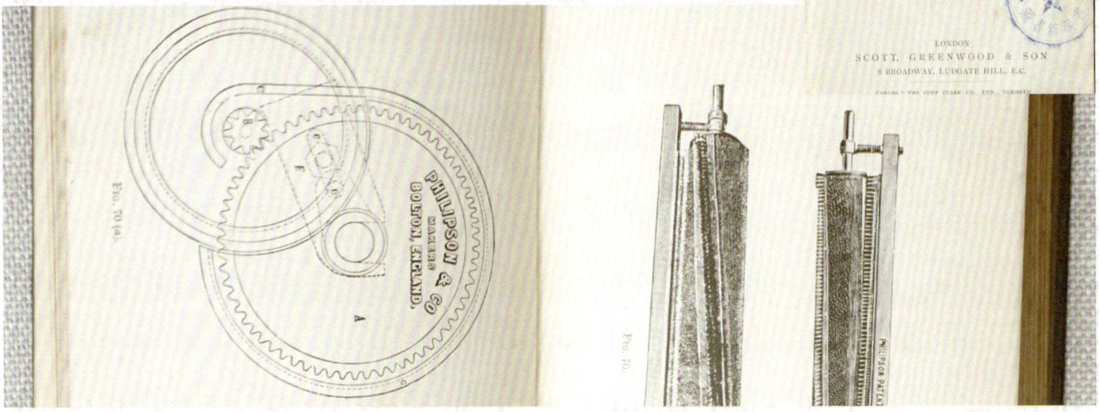

Cotton Spinning Calculation

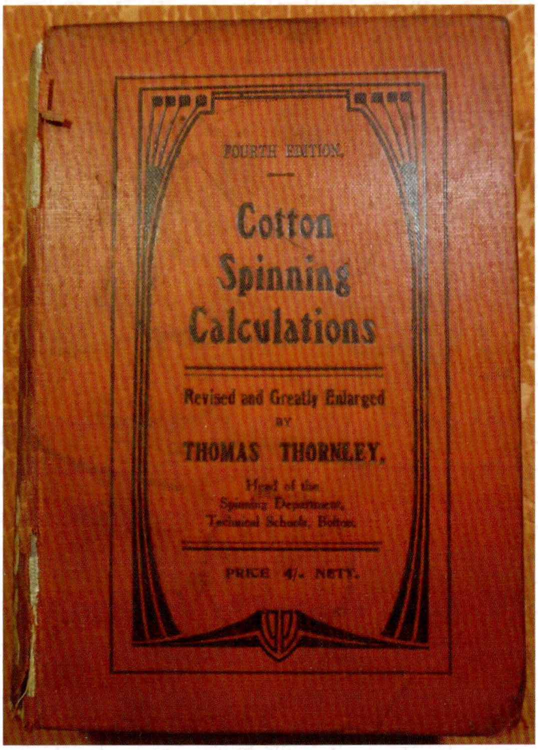

著者：THOMAS THORNLEY

出版者：JOHN HEYWOOD LTD. MANCHESTER

出版时间：1911 年

历史馆藏：青岛守备军民政部、青岛工学院

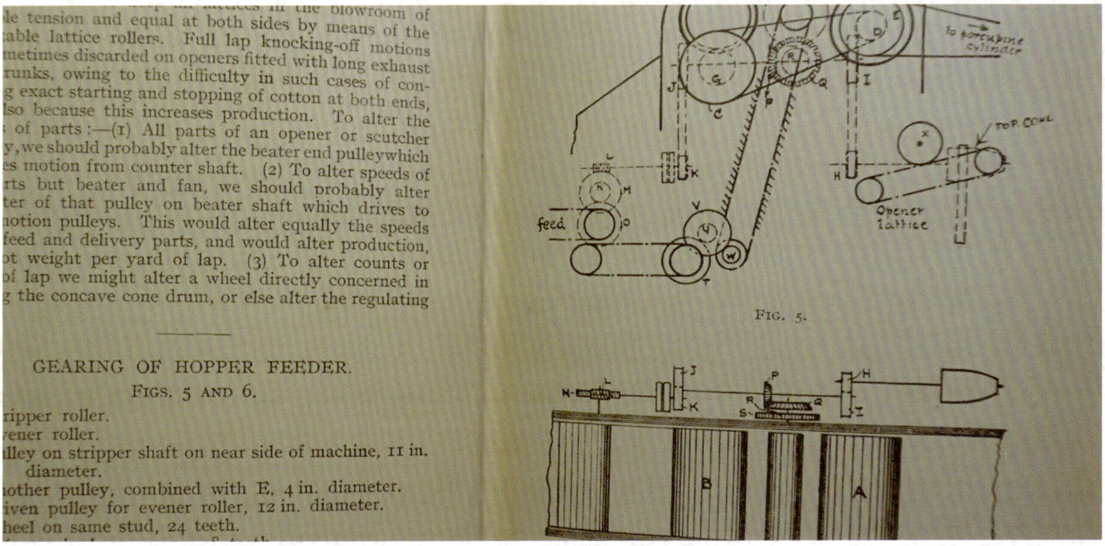

The Cotton Plant in Egypt

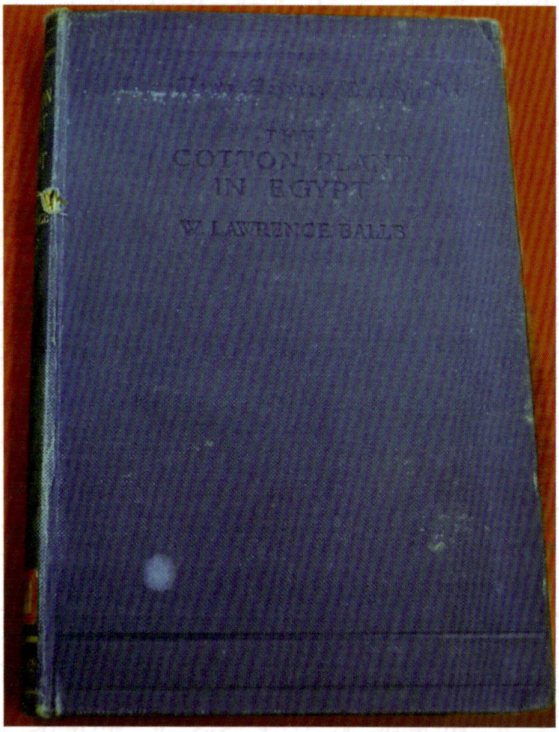

著者：W. Lawrence Balls
出版者：MacMillan and Co., Ltd.
出版时间：1912 年
历史馆藏：校友捐赠

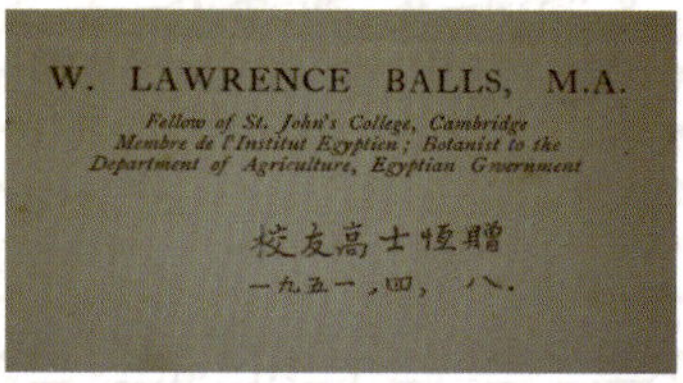
W. LAWRENCE BALLS, M.A.

Fellow of St. John's College, Cambridge
Membre de l'Institut Egyptien; Botanist to the
Department of Agriculture, Egyptian Government

校友高士恒赠
一九五一，四，八.

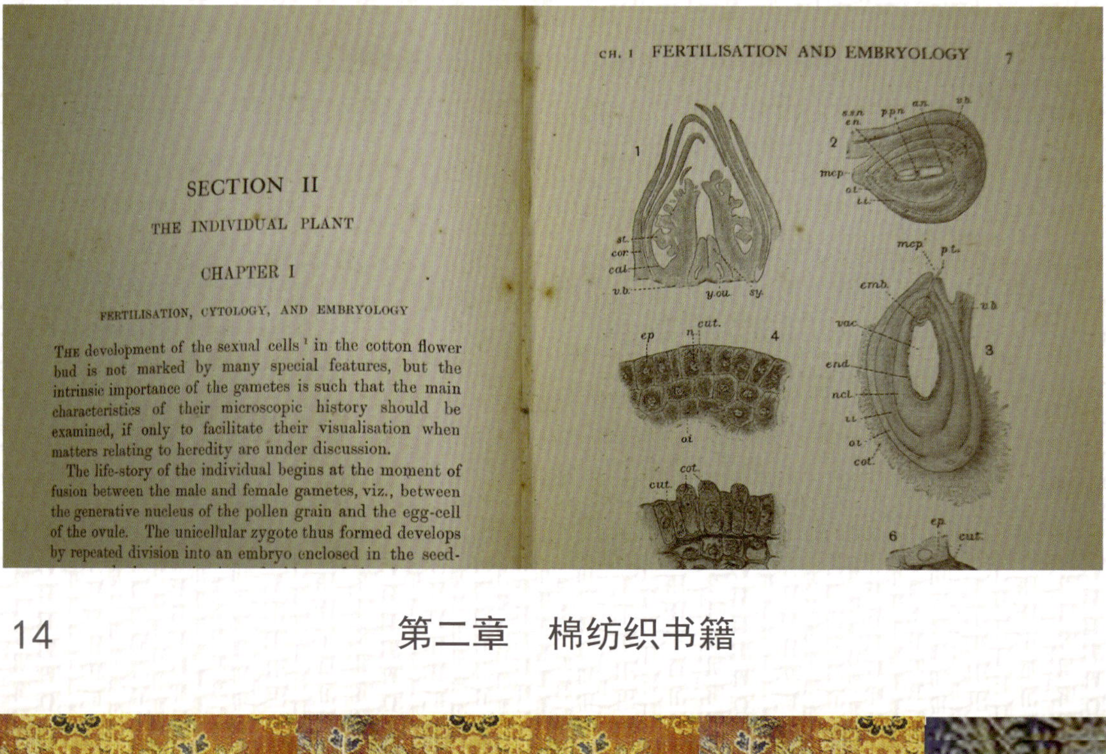
SECTION II

THE INDIVIDUAL PLANT

CHAPTER I

FERTILISATION, CYTOLOGY, AND EMBRYOLOGY

THE development of the sexual cells[1] in the cotton flower bud is not marked by many special features, but the intrinsic importance of the gametes is such that the main characteristics of their microscopic history should be examined, if only to facilitate their visualisation when matters relating to heredity are under discussion.

The life-story of the individual begins at the moment of fusion between the male and female gametes, viz., between the generative nucleus of the pollen grain and the egg-cell of the ovule. The unicellular zygote thus formed develops by repeated division into an embryo enclosed in the seed-

CH. I FERTILISATION AND EMBRYOLOGY 7

Fine Cotton Spinning

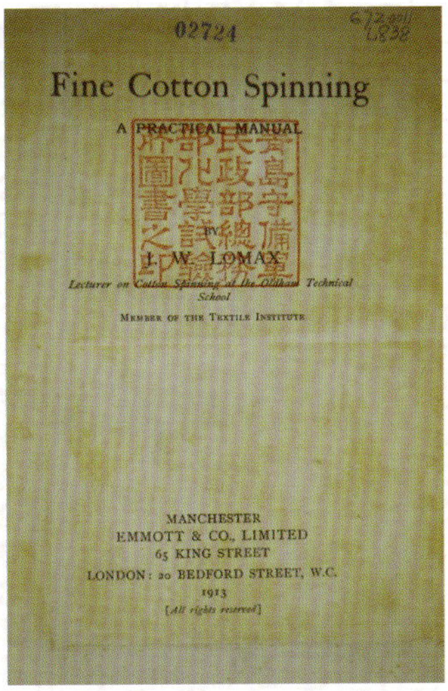

02724

Fine Cotton Spinning

A PRACTICAL MANUAL

BY

J. W. LOMAX

Lecturer on Cotton Spinning at the Oldham Technical School

Member of the Textile Institute

MANCHESTER
EMMOTT & CO., LIMITED
65 KING STREET
LONDON: 20 BEDFORD STREET, W.C.
1913
[All rights reserved]

著者：J. W. Lomax
出版者：Manchester Emmott & Co., Ltd.
出版时间：1913 年
历史馆藏：青岛守备军民政部、青岛工学院

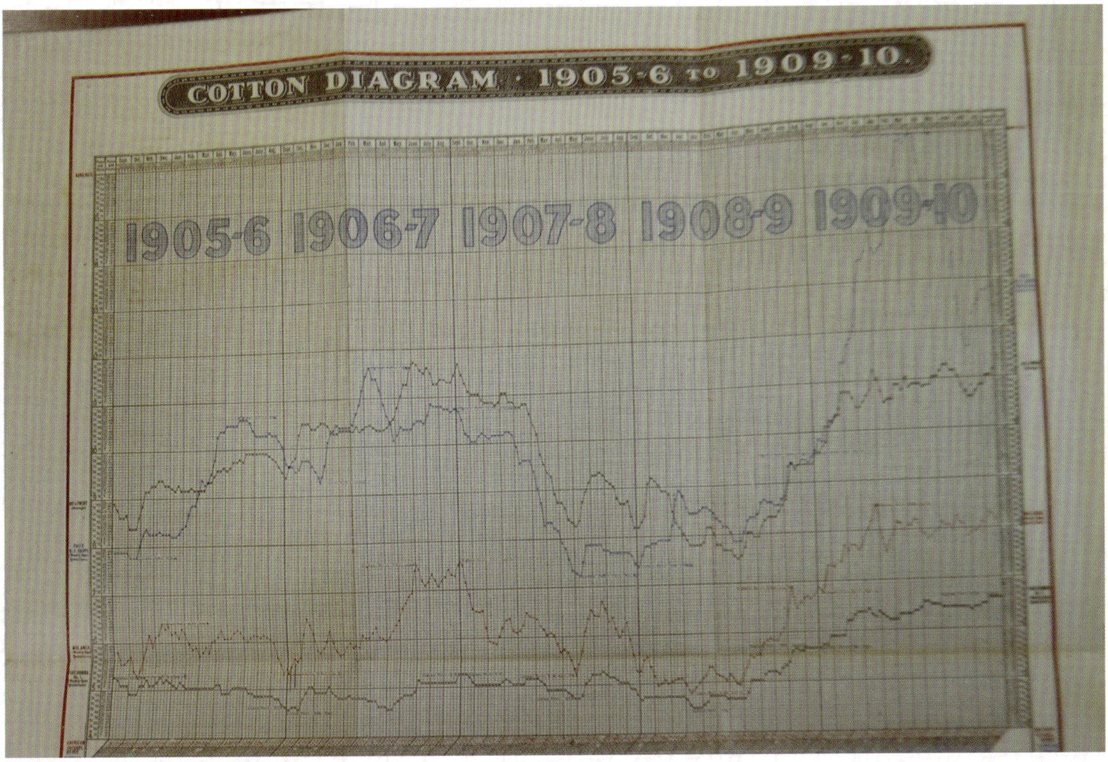

Cotton Doubling and Twisting

著者：Sam Wakefield　　　　出版时间：1915 年
出版者：Masden & Co., Ltd.　历史馆藏：青岛守备军民政部、青岛工学院

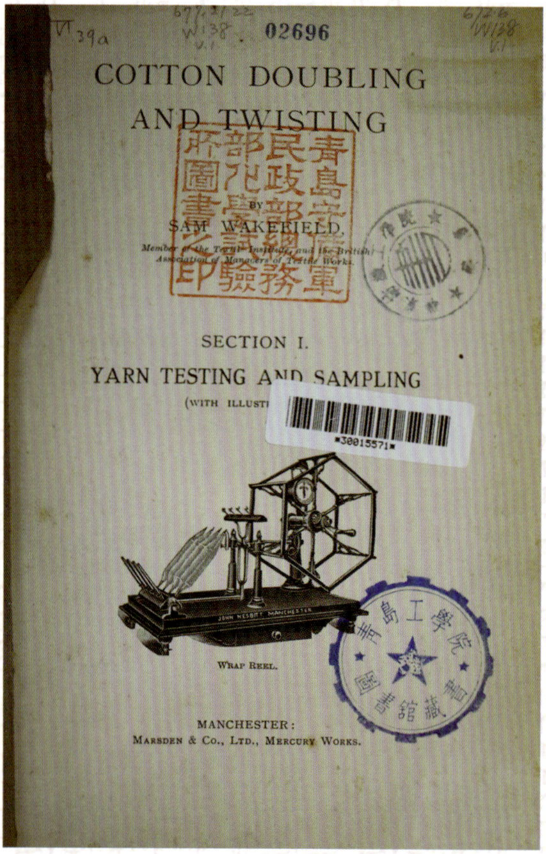

A Method of Determining Costs in a Cotton Mill

著者：Henry W. Nichols
出版者：Anthony & Sons, Inc.
出版时间：1915 年
历史馆藏：南通纺织专门学校

The Cotton Year Book

出版者：Textile Mercury,LTD.
出版时间：1918 年起　　　　历史馆藏：南通学院

The Indian Cotton Textile Industry

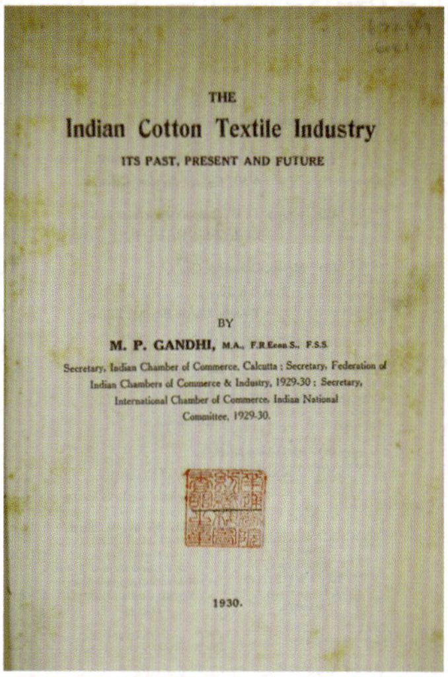

著者：M. P. Gandhi
出版者：The Book Company, Ltd.
出版时间：1930 年
历史馆藏：南通学院

中国之棉纺织业

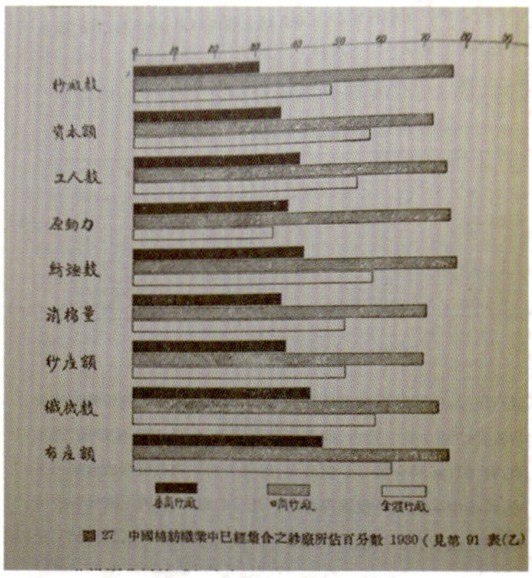

编者：方显廷
出版者：国立编译馆
出版时间：1934 年
历史馆藏：私立上海纺织工业专科学校

Cotton Combing

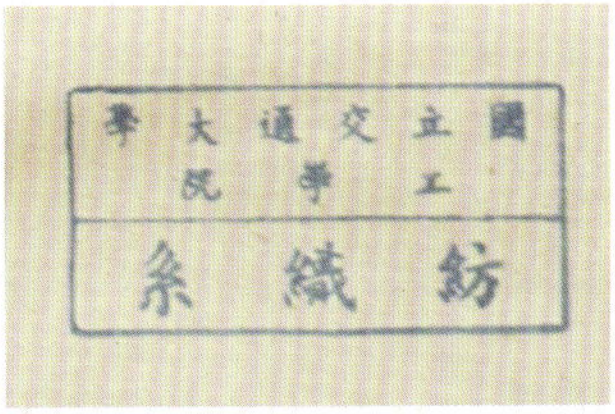

著者：GILBERT R.MERRILL　　出版者：Pawtucket, Rhode Island
出版时间：1936 年　　历史馆藏：国立交通大学

中国棉业问题

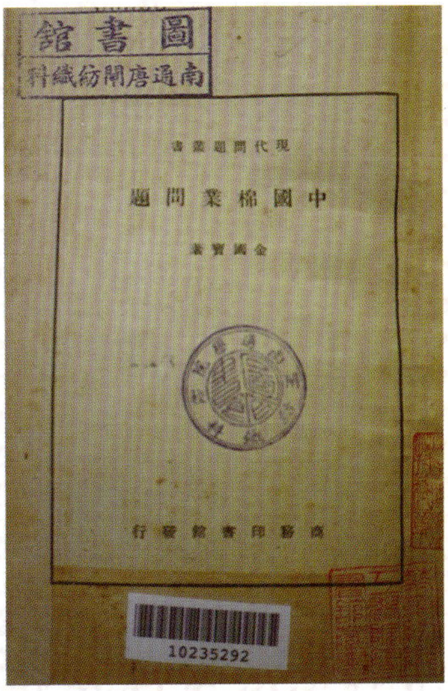

著者：金国宝
出版者：商务印书馆
出版时间：1937 年
历史馆藏：南通学院

Cotton Spinning

著者：Willis, Dunlap and Moore
出版者：The Textile Foundation
出版时间：1938 年

棉纺机械计算学

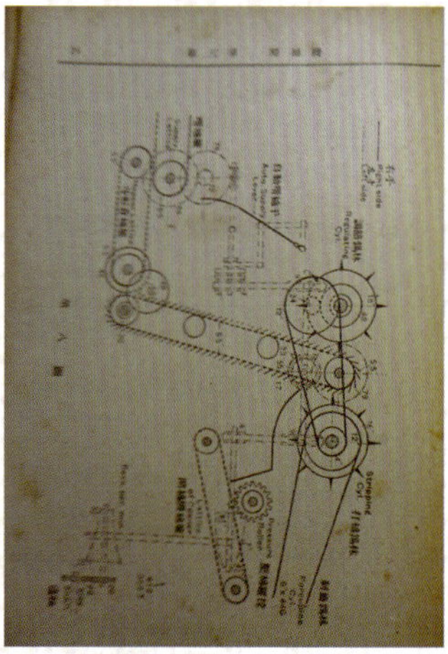

编者：唐仁杰
出版者：中国纺织染工业补习学校
出版时间：1940 年
历史馆藏：苏州工业学校、苏南工专

Worsted Spinner's Practical Handbook

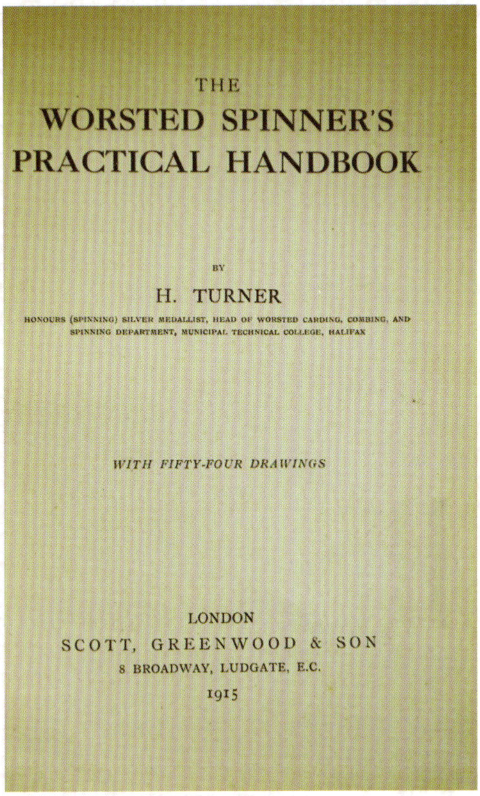

THE
WORSTED SPINNER'S
PRACTICAL HANDBOOK

BY

H. TURNER

HONOURS (SPINNING) SILVER MEDALLIST, HEAD OF WORSTED CARDING, COMBING, AND SPINNING DEPARTMENT, MUNICIPAL TECHNICAL COLLEGE, HALIFAX

WITH FIFTY-FOUR DRAWINGS

LONDON
SCOTT, GREENWOOD & SON
8 BROADWAY, LUDGATE, E.C.
1915

著者：H. Turner
出版者：Scott, Greenwood & Son
出版时间：1915 年

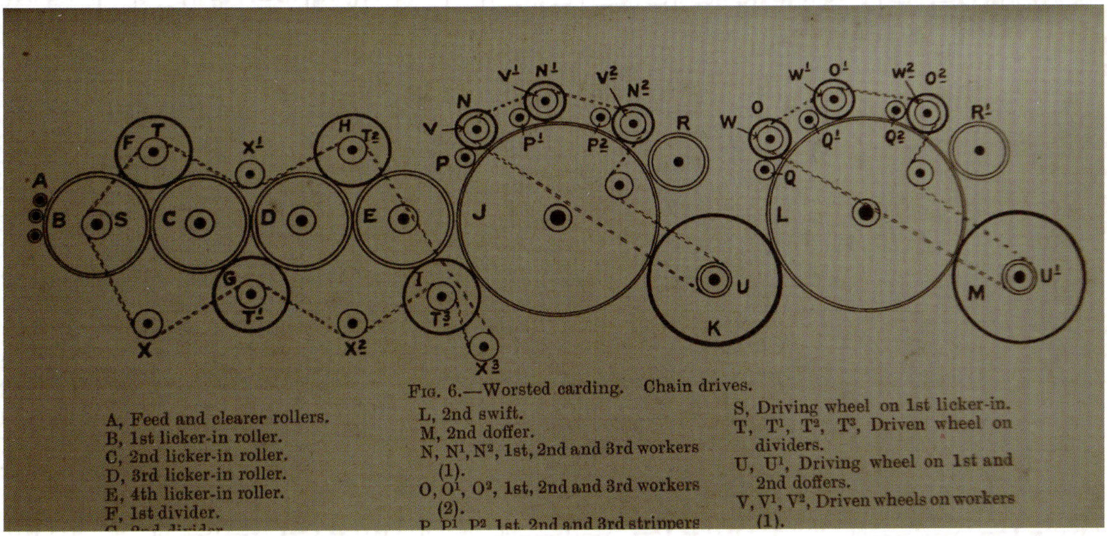

FIG. 6.—Worsted carding. Chain drives.

A, Feed and clearer rollers.
B, 1st licker-in roller.
C, 2nd licker-in roller.
D, 3rd licker-in roller.
E, 4th licker-in roller.
F, 1st divider.

L, 2nd swift.
M, 2nd doffer.
N, N^1, N^2, 1st, 2nd and 3rd workers (1).
O, O^1, O^2, 1st, 2nd and 3rd workers (2).
P, P^1, P^2 1st, 2nd and 3rd strippers

S, Driving wheel on 1st licker-in.
T, T^1, T^2, T^3, Driven wheel on dividers.
U, U^1, Driving wheel on 1st and 2nd doffers.
V, V^1, V^2, Driven wheels on workers (1).

Wool

著者：FRANK ORMEROD
出版者：HENRY HOLT AND COMPANY
出版时间：1919 年
历史馆藏：国立上海理工学院

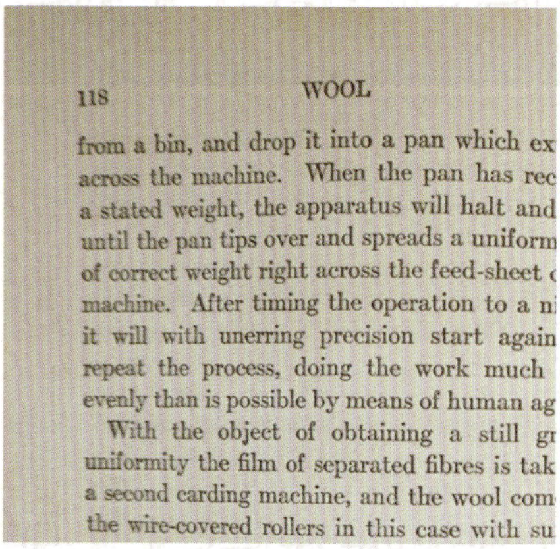
118 WOOL

from a bin, and drop it into a pan which ex
across the machine. When the pan has rec
a stated weight, the apparatus will halt and
until the pan tips over and spreads a uniform
of correct weight right across the feed-sheet c
machine. After timing the operation to a ni
it will with unerring precision start again
repeat the process, doing the work much
evenly than is possible by means of human ag
With the object of obtaining a still gr
uniformity the film of separated fibres is tak
a second carding machine, and the wool com
the wire-covered rollers in this case with su

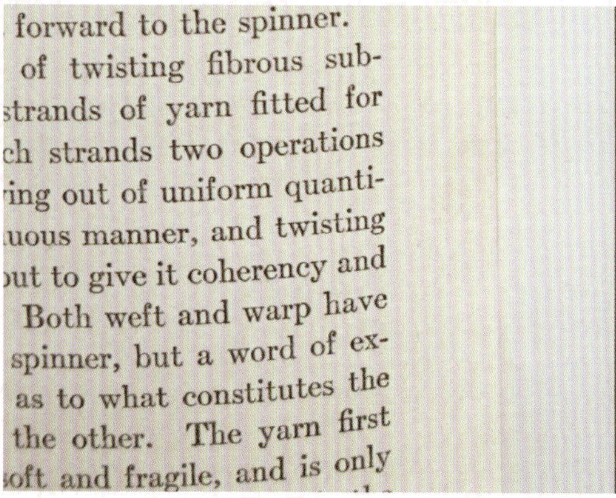
forward to the spinner.
of twisting fibrous sub-
strands of yarn fitted for
ch strands two operations
ing out of uniform quanti-
uous manner, and twisting
out to give it coherency and
Both weft and warp have
spinner, but a word of ex-
as to what constitutes the
the other. The yarn first
soft and fragile, and is only

Woollen and Worsted Industries

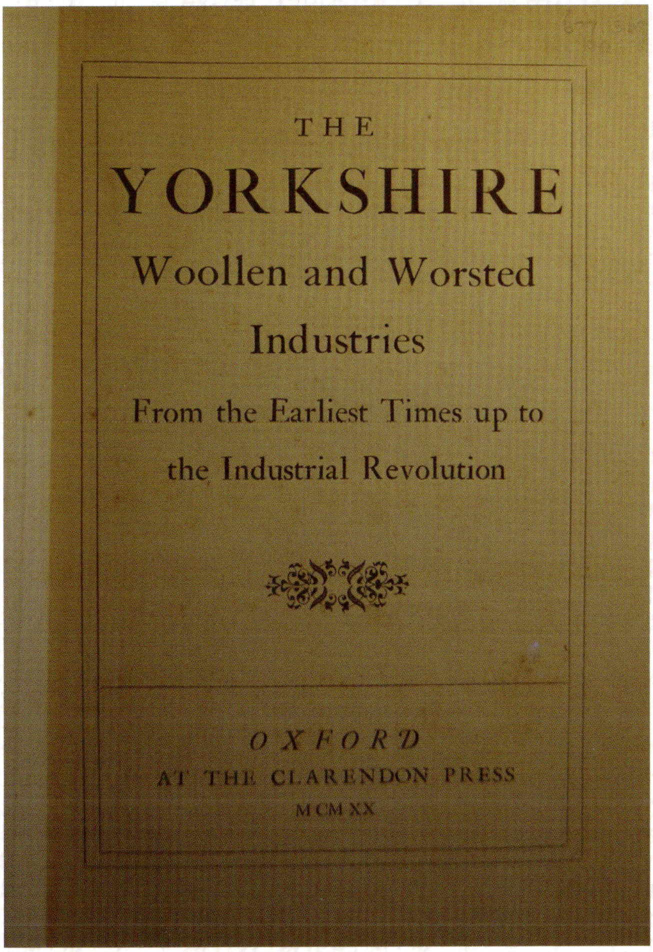

著者：HERBERT HEATON
出版者：OXFORD UNIVERSITY PRESS
出版时间：1920 年
历史馆藏：交通大学

Woollen and Worsted

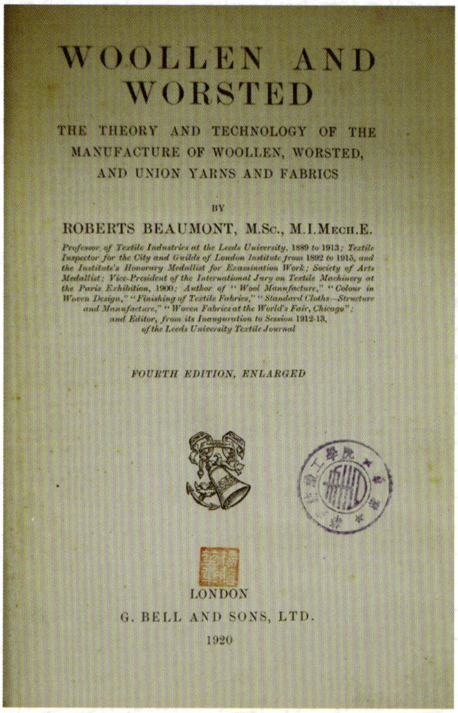

WOOLLEN AND WORSTED

THE THEORY AND TECHNOLOGY OF THE MANUFACTURE OF WOOLLEN, WORSTED, AND UNION YARNS AND FABRICS

BY

ROBERTS BEAUMONT, M.Sc., M.I.Mech.E.

Professor of Textile Industries at the Leeds University, 1889 to 1913; Textile Inspector for the City and Guilds of London Institute from 1892 to 1915, and the Institute's Honorary Medallist for Examination Work; Society of Arts Medallist; Vice-President of the International Jury on Textile Machinery at the Paris Exhibition, 1900; Author of "Wool Manufacture," "Colour in Woven Design," "Finishing of Textile Fabrics," "Standard Cloths—Structure and Manufacture," "Woven Fabrics at the World's Fair, Chicago"; and Editor, from its Inauguration to Session 1912-13, of the Leeds University Textile Journal

FOURTH EDITION, ENLARGED

LONDON

G. BELL AND SONS, LTD.

1920

著者：Roberts Beaumont
出版者：G. Bell and Sons, Ltd.
出版时间：1920 年
历史馆藏：校友捐赠

Worsted Cone Drawing

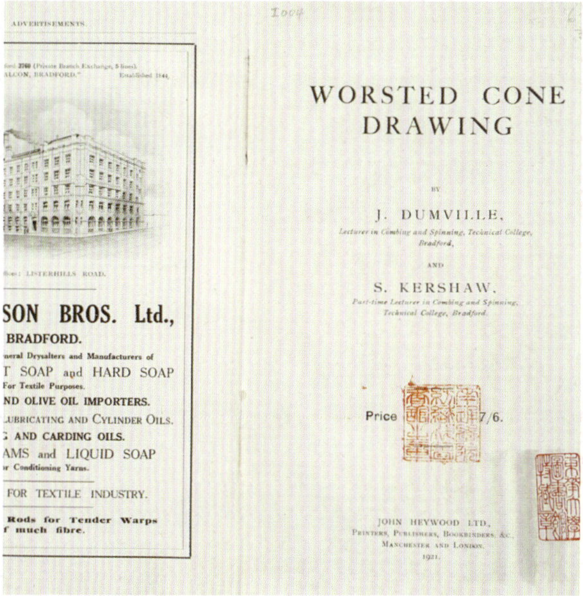

著者：J. DUMVILLE AND S.KERSHAW
出版者：JOHN HEYWOOD LTD.
出版时间：1921 年
历史馆藏：南通学院

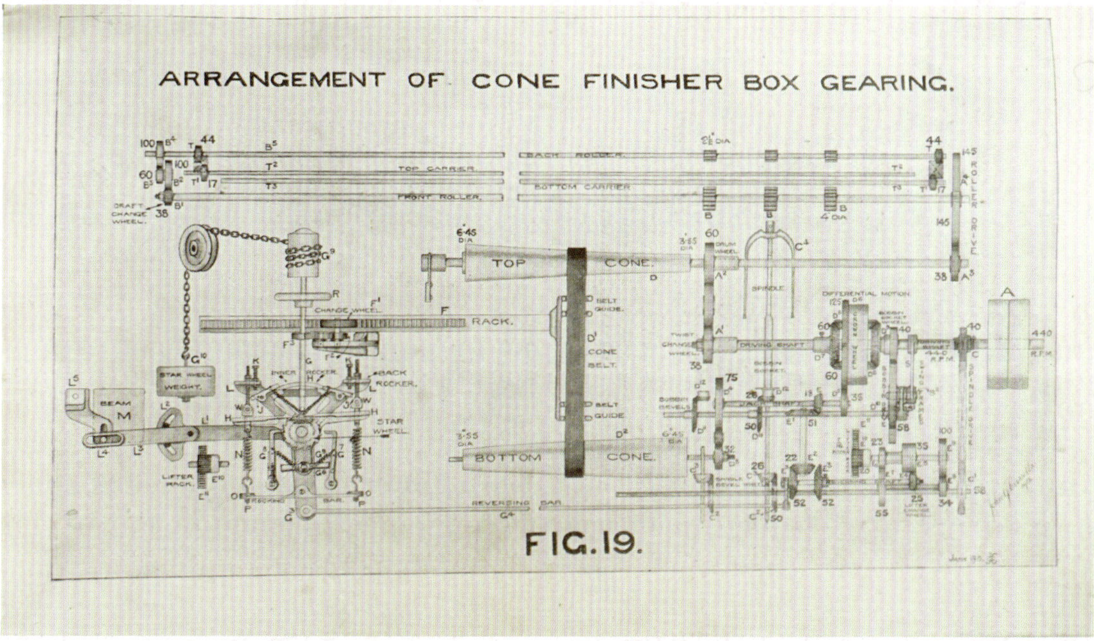

Wool Carding

编者： JAMES BRADLEY
出版者：EMMOTT & CO., LIMITED
出版时间：1921 年
历史馆藏：交通大学

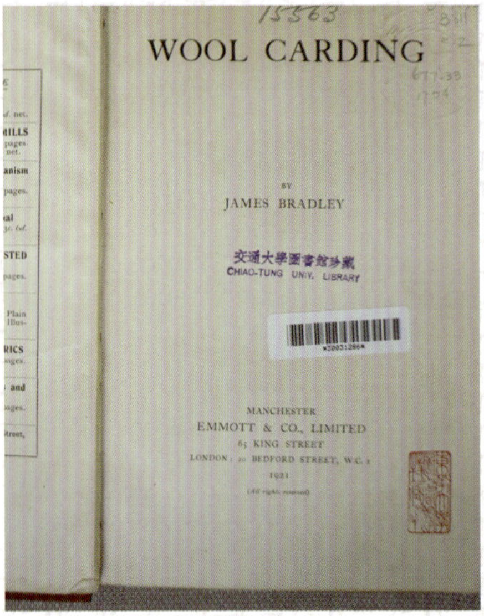

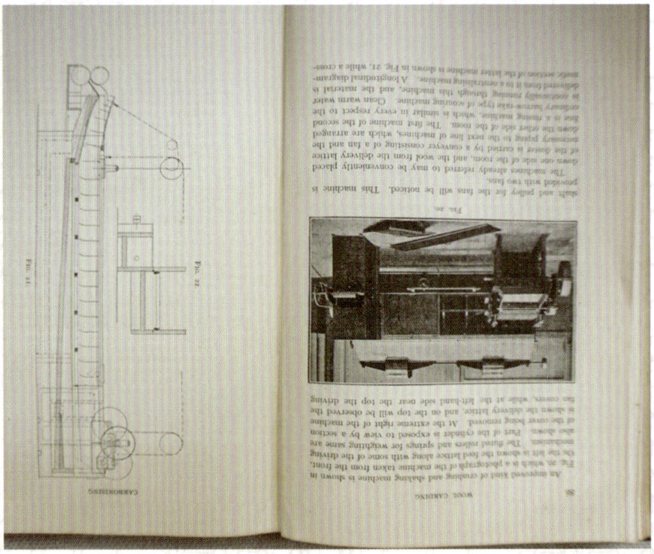

Woollen and Worsted Spinning

著者：ALDRED F. BARKER
出版者：CASSELL AND COMPANY, LTD.
出版时间：1922 年
历史馆藏：南通学院

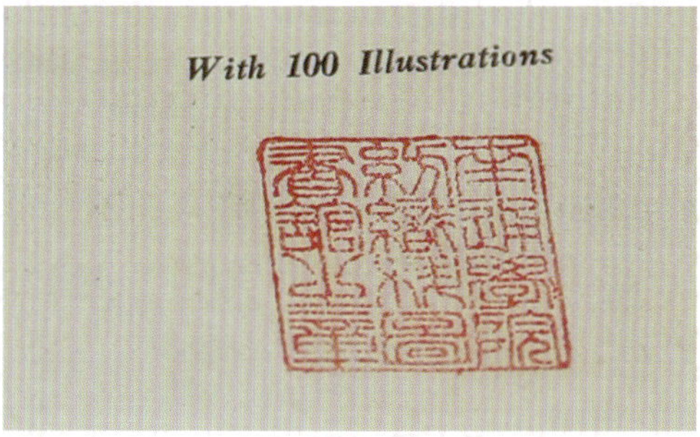

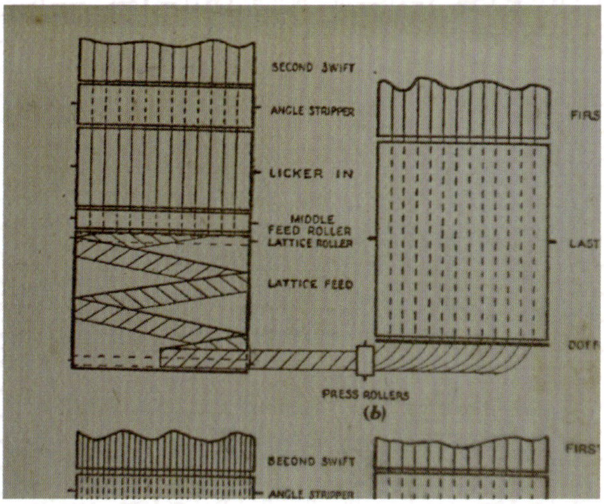

Wool Substitutes

编者：ROBERTS BEAUMONT
出版者：SIR ISAAC PITMAN & SONS, LTD.
出版时间：1922 年
历史馆藏：交通大学

WOOL
SUBSTITUTES

BY
ROBERTS BEAUMONT
M.Sc., M.Inst.Mech.E.

Author of "Woollen and Worsted," "Colour in Woven Design," "Union Textile Fabrication," "Standard Cloths," "Finishing of Textile Fabrics," etc.

Professor of Textile Industries, Leeds University, 1889 to 1913; Clothworkers' Inspector of Textile Schools in Great Britain and Ireland, 1892 to 1916; Examiner's Medallist, City and Guilds of London Institute; Royal Society of Arts Medallist; Acting President of the International Jury on Textile Machinery, Paris Exhibition, 1900, etc.

LONDON
SIR ISAAC PITMAN & SONS, LTD.
PARKER STREET, KINGSWAY, W.C.2
BATH, MELBOURNE, TORONTO, NEW YORK
1922

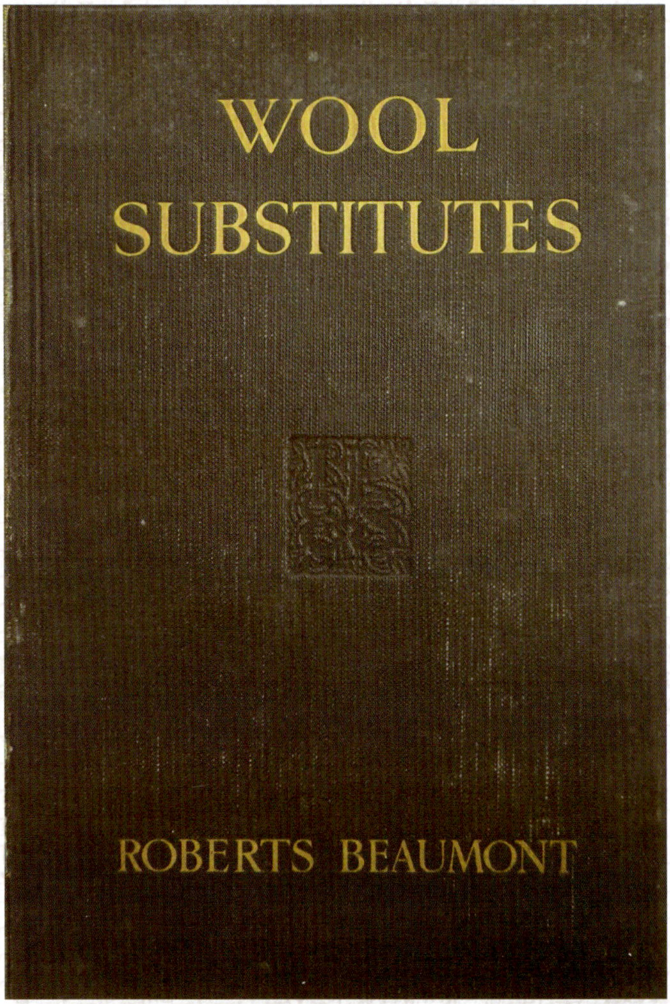

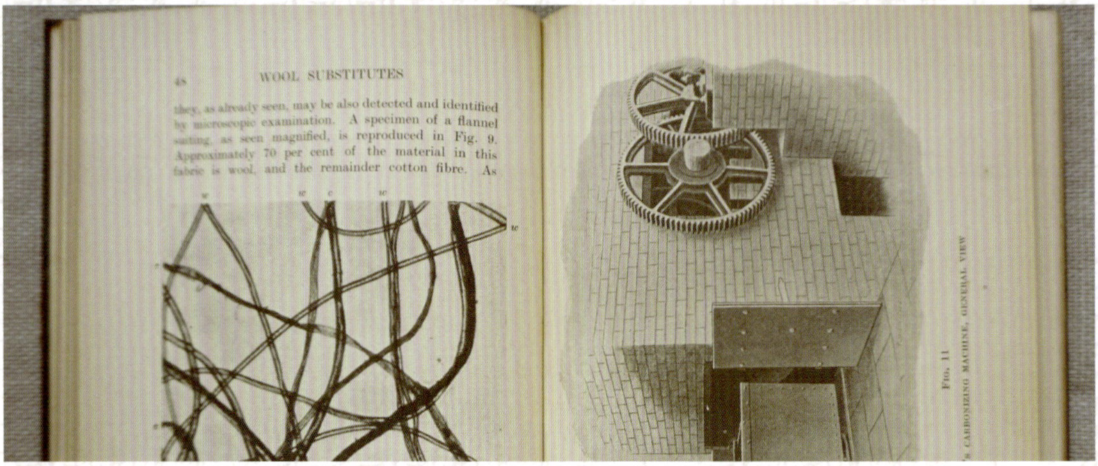

WOOL SUBSTITUTES

they, as already seen, may be also detected and identified by microscopic examination. A specimen of a flannel suiting, as seen magnified, is reproduced in Fig. 9. Approximately 70 per cent of the material in this fabric is wool, and the remainder cotton fibre. As

Worsted Preparing and Spinning

著者：FRED BRADBURY
出版者：F. KING & SONS, LTD.
出版时间：1922 年
历史馆藏：交通大学

Woollen Yarn Production

著者：T. LAWSON
出版者： SIR ISAAC
PTTMAN & SONS,LTD.
出版时间：1924 年
历史馆藏：南通学院

The American Wool Manufacture

著者：HARRISON COLE　　出版者：HARVARD UNIVERSITY PRESS
出版时间：1926 年　　历史馆藏：南通学院

Worsted Open Drawing

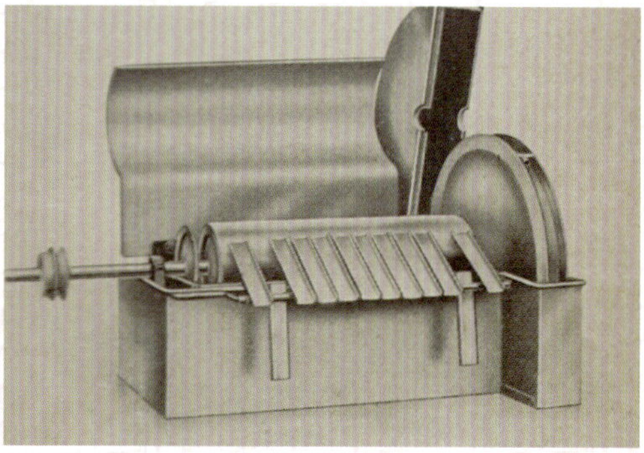

著者：S.KERSHAW, F.T.I.
出版者：SIR ISAAC PITMAN & SONS, LTD.
出版时间：1931 年
历史馆藏：南通学院、交通大学

Jute and Linen Weaving

著者：Thomas Woodhouse Thomas Milne
出版者：LONGMANS,GREEN AND CO. LTD.
出版时间：1906 年
历史馆藏：苏南工专、苏州工业学校

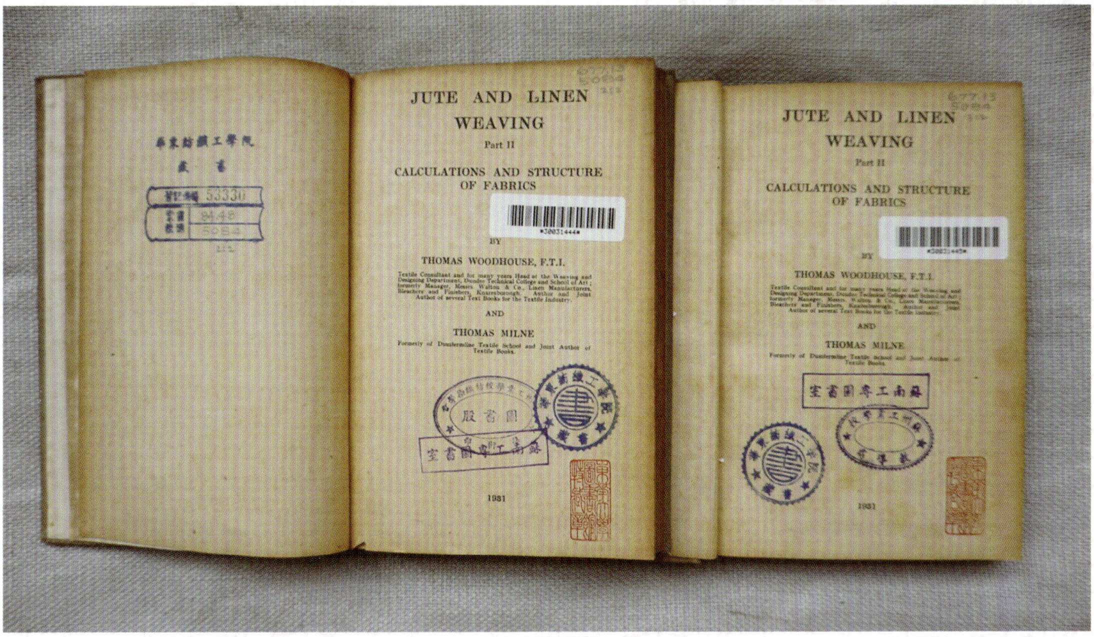

Modern Flax, Hemp, and Jute Spinning and Twisting

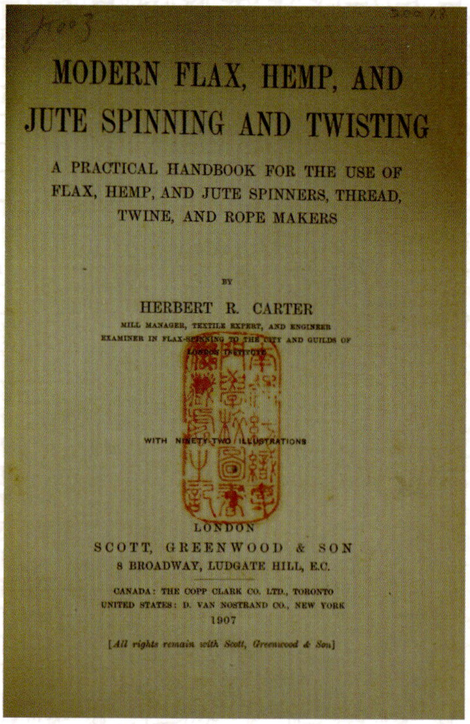

MODERN FLAX, HEMP, AND JUTE SPINNING AND TWISTING

A PRACTICAL HANDBOOK FOR THE USE OF FLAX, HEMP, AND JUTE SPINNERS, THREAD, TWINE, AND ROPE MAKERS

BY

HERBERT R. CARTER

MILL MANAGER, TEXTILE EXPERT, AND ENGINEER
EXAMINER IN FLAX-SPINNING TO THE CITY AND GUILDS OF LONDON INSTITUTE

WITH NINETY-TWO ILLUSTRATIONS

LONDON
SCOTT, GREENWOOD & SON
8 BROADWAY, LUDGATE HILL, E.C.

CANADA: THE COPP CLARK CO. LTD., TORONTO
UNITED STATES: D. VAN NOSTRAND CO., NEW YORK
1907

[*All rights remain with Scott, Greenwood & Son*]

著者：Herbert R. Carter
出版者：Scott, Greenwood & Son
出版时间：1907 年
历史馆藏：南通纺织专门学校

Fig. 25.—Special short fibre card with hopper feed.

The Finising of Jute and Linen Fabrics

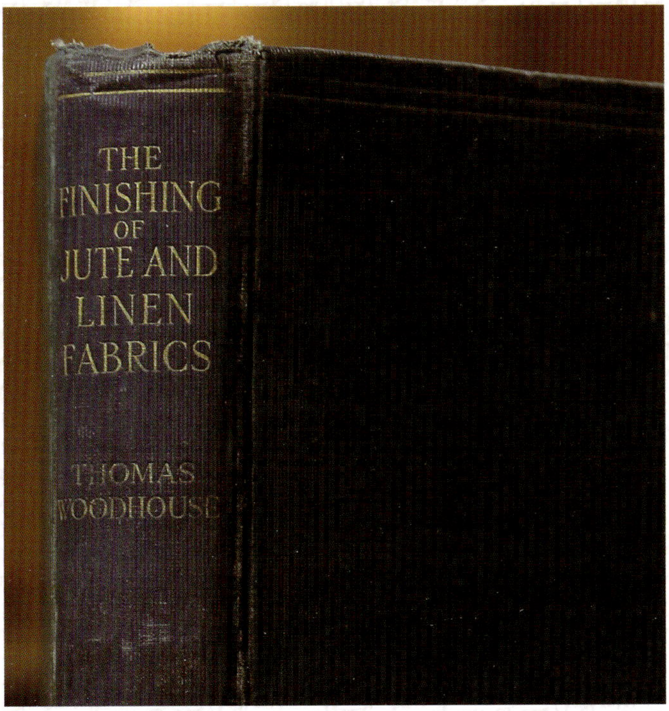

编者：Thomas Woodhouse Macmillan
出版者：LONDON SIR ISAAC PITMAN & SONS, LTD.
出版时间：1914 年
历史馆藏：南通学院

The Jute Industry

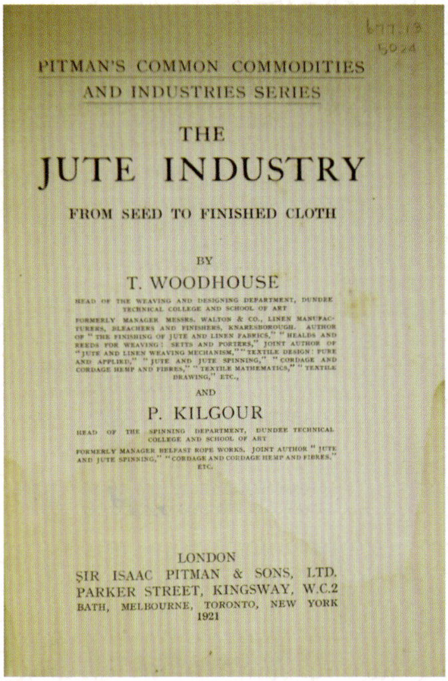
PITMAN'S COMMON COMMODITIES
AND INDUSTRIES SERIES

THE
JUTE INDUSTRY
FROM SEED TO FINISHED CLOTH

BY
T. WOODHOUSE
HEAD OF THE WEAVING AND DESIGNING DEPARTMENT, DUNDEE TECHNICAL COLLEGE AND SCHOOL OF ART
FORMERLY MANAGER MESSRS. WALTON & CO., LINEN MANUFACTURERS, BLEACHERS AND FINISHERS, KNARESBOROUGH. AUTHOR OF "THE FINISHING OF JUTE AND LINEN FABRICS," "HEALDS AND REEDS FOR WEAVING: SETTS AND PORTERS," JOINT AUTHOR OF "JUTE AND LINEN WEAVING MECHANISM," "TEXTILE DESIGN: PURE AND APPLIED," "JUTE AND JUTE SPINNING," "CORDAGE AND CORDAGE HEMP AND FIBRES," "TEXTILE MATHEMATICS," "TEXTILE DRAWING," ETC.,

AND
P. KILGOUR
HEAD OF THE SPINNING DEPARTMENT, DUNDEE TECHNICAL COLLEGE AND SCHOOL OF ART
FORMERLY MANAGER BELFAST ROPE WORKS. JOINT AUTHOR "JUTE AND JUTE SPINNING," "CORDAGE AND CORDAGE HEMP AND FIBRES," ETC.

LONDON
SIR ISAAC PITMAN & SONS, LTD.
PARKER STREET, KINGSWAY, W.C.2
BATH, MELBOURNE, TORONTO, NEW YORK
1921

著者：T. Woodhouse, P. Kilgour
出版者：Sir Isaac Pitman & Sons, Ltd.
出版时间：1921 年
历史馆藏：NYU

FIG. 29
WINDING-ON OR DRY BEAMING MACHINE

Spinning Weaving and Finishing of Flax and Jute

著者：THOMAS WOODHOUSE
出版者：SIR ISAAC PITMAN & SONS, LTD.
出版时间：1929 年
历史馆藏：交通大学

Jute Spinning Calculations

著者：Andrew Smith
出版者：Sir Isaac Pitman & Sons, Ltd.
出版时间：1935 年
历史馆藏：私立中国纺织工学院

制麻

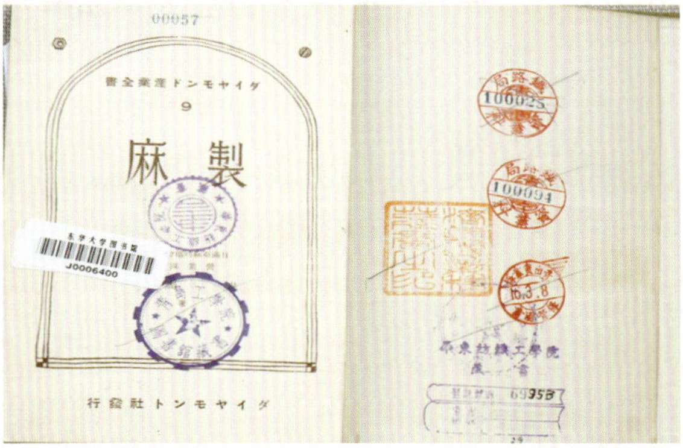

著者：森周一
出版者：日满亚麻纺织会社
出版时间：1938 年
历史馆藏：青岛工学院、济南铁路局

麻再编成

著者：森周一　　出版者：日本纤维研究会刊
出版时间：1942 年　　历史馆藏：诚孚纺织专科学校

The Structure of the Wool Fibre

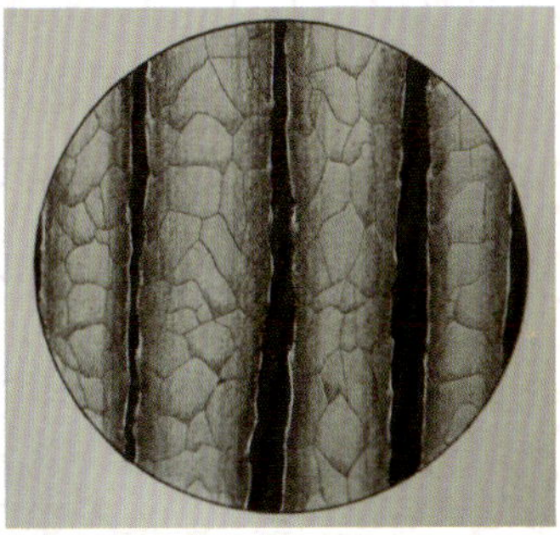

著者：F. H. Bowman
出版者：MacMillan and Co., Ltd.
出版时间：1908 年
历史馆藏：南通学院

The Production of Cotton

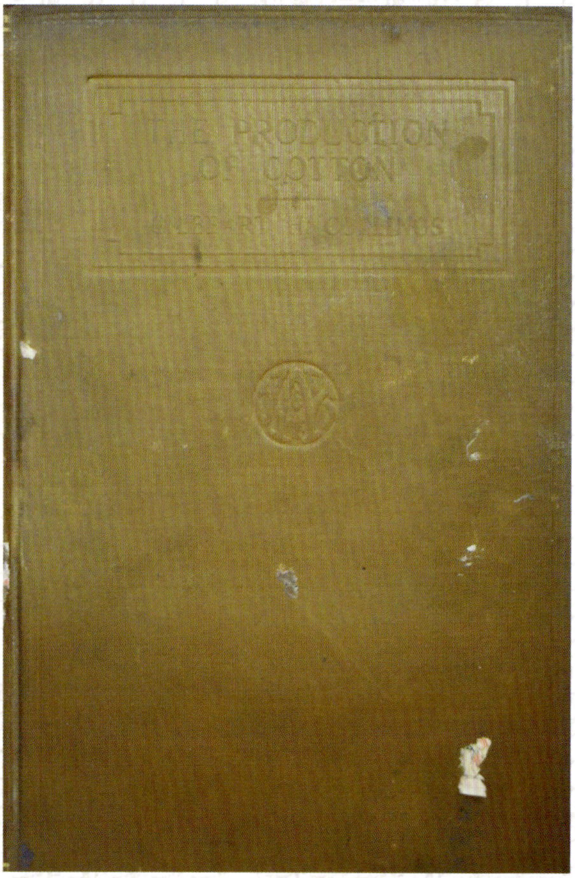

著者：Gilbeart H. Collings　　出版者：John Willey & Sons, Inc.
出版时间：1926 年　　历史馆藏：南通学院

should be used, and the speed of the gin should be regulated so that it will not be too rapid. Farmers should insist that the ginneries be equipped with good machinery before they allow their cotton to be ginned. Poor machinery used in ginning increases the amount of linters and decreases the amount of lint.

Types of Ginneries. — There are two types of ginneries: (1) one-story ginneries; and (2) two-story ginneries. The fire risk is not so great with one-story buildings, and of course, the insurance is less. Also, the vibration is less with the one-story buildings, and consequently less wear and tear on the machinery. Good, substantial, fireproof two-story ginneries can be built, however.

Types of Cotton Gins. — The kind of gin used will depend upon the kind of cotton to be ginned. There are two types of cotton gins. First, we have what is known as the saw gin, the principle of which is the same as the gin first invented by Eli Whitney. The cotton is fed into a hopper, one side of which is a grate or grid. Through this grid a number of thin steel saws revolve. These saws are usually 10 or 12 inches in diameter, and number from 40 to 80. The teeth of the saws, as they revolve, catch in the fiber and pull the fiber from the seeds, as the grids are so set that the seeds cannot be pulled through. The saws are cleaned of the ginned fiber by revolving brushes. The saw gin can be used satisfactorily to gin Upland cotton, both the long and the short staple. This gin cannot be used to gin Sea Island and American-Egyptian cotton for it breaks their long fibers. Even a small percentage of the fibers of the Upland cotton is broken under the best of conditions, and the percentage may be greatly increased if the gin is run too rapidly, or if the cotton is fed too fast, or if the cotton is not dry when ginned.

Second, we have the roller gin, which is used in ginning Sea Island and American-Egyptian cotton. The roller gin was brought into this

compared with the quantity of Upland cotton ginned per hour by the saw gin. This greater time demanded in ginning 500 pounds of Sea Island or American-Egyptian cotton, as compared with the time required in ginning 500 pounds of Upland, results in the greater charges for ginning the long staples.

Fig. 73. — Cotton bales lying in field around wooden shed. (Courtesy, U. S. Dept. of Agriculture.)

At one time there was a movement started to operate traveling gins which were owned by individual corporations, or coöperatively among the farmers, just as some threshing machines are owned today. However, this never proved successful, one of the chief objections being the

Textile Fibers and Their Use

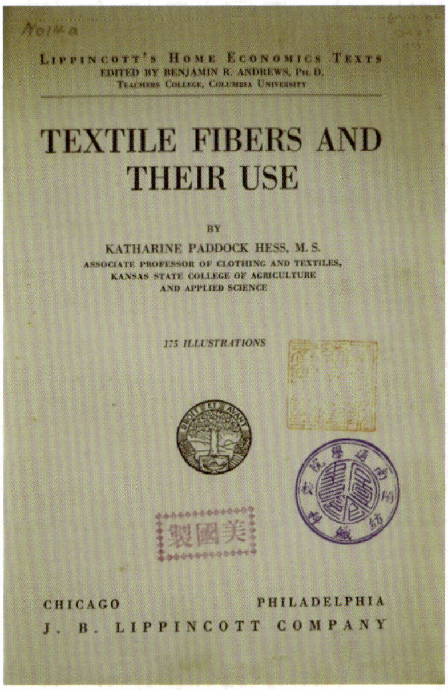

LIPPINCOTT'S HOME ECONOMICS TEXTS
EDITED BY BENJAMIN R. ANDREWS, PH. D.
TEACHERS COLLEGE, COLUMBIA UNIVERSITY

TEXTILE FIBERS AND THEIR USE

BY

KATHARINE PADDOCK HESS, M. S.
ASSOCIATE PROFESSOR OF CLOTHING AND TEXTILES, KANSAS STATE COLLEGE OF AGRICULTURE AND APPLIED SCIENCE

175 ILLUSTRATIONS

美國製

CHICAGO PHILADELPHIA
J. B. LIPPINCOTT COMPANY

著者：Katharine Paddock Hess
出版者：J.B.LIPPINCOTT COMPANY
出版时间：1931 年
历史馆藏：南通学院

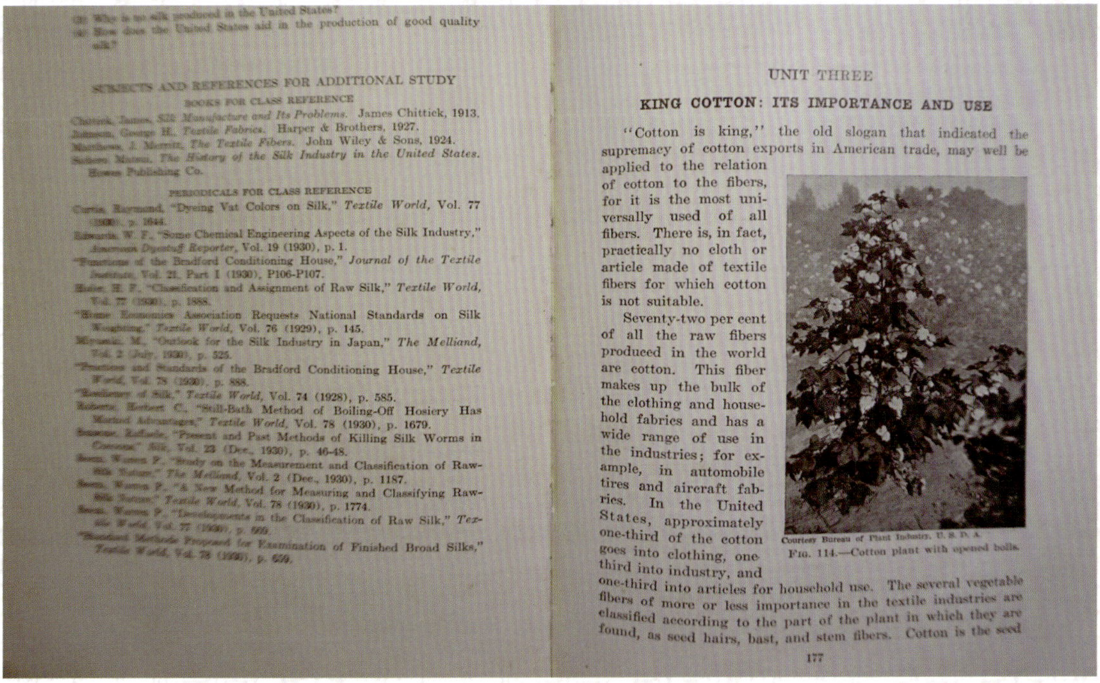

(3) Why is no silk produced in the United States?
(4) How does the United States aid in the production of good quality silk?

SUBJECTS AND REFERENCES FOR ADDITIONAL STUDY

BOOKS FOR CLASS REFERENCE

Chittick, James, *Silk Manufacture and Its Problems.* James Chittick, 1913.
Johnson, George H., *Textile Fabrics.* Harper & Brothers, 1927.
Matthews, J. Merritt, *The Textile Fibers.* John Wiley & Sons, 1924.
Seibert, Mason, *The History of the Silk Industry in the United States.* Howes Publishing Co.

PERIODICALS FOR CLASS REFERENCE

Curtis, Raymond, "Dyeing Vat Colors on Silk," *Textile World,* Vol. 77 (1930), p. 1644.
Edwards, W. F., "Some Chemical Engineering Aspects of the Silk Industry," *American Dyestuff Reporter,* Vol. 19 (1930), p. 1.
"Functions of the Bradford Conditioning House," *Journal of the Textile Institute,* Vol. 21, Part I (1930), P106-P107.
Hobe, H. F., "Classification and Assignment of Raw Silk," *Textile World,* Vol. 77 (1930), p. 1888.
"Home Economics Association Requests National Standards on Silk Weighting," *Textile World,* Vol. 76 (1929), p. 145.
Miyazaki, M., "Outlook for the Silk Industry in Japan," *The Melliand,* Vol. 2 (July, 1930), p. 525.
"Practices and Standards of the Bradford Conditioning House," *Textile World,* Vol. 78 (1930), p. 888.
"Resiliency of Silk," *Textile World,* Vol. 74 (1928), p. 585.
Roberts, Herbert C., "Still-Bath Method of Boiling-Off Hosiery Has Marked Advantages," *Textile World,* Vol. 78 (1930), p. 1679.
Sessa, Raffaele, "Present and Past Methods of Killing Silk Worms in Cocoons," *Silk,* Vol. 23 (Dec., 1930), p. 46-48.
Seem, Warren P., "Study on the Measurement and Classification of Raw-Silk Nature," *The Melliand,* Vol. 2 (Dec., 1930), p. 1187.
Seem, Warren P., "A New Method for Measuring and Classifying Raw-Silk Nature," *Textile World,* Vol. 78 (1930), p. 1774.
Seem, Warren P., "Developments in the Classification of Raw Silk," *Textile World,* Vol. 77 (1930), p. 699.
"Standard Methods Proposed for Examination of Finished Broad Silks," *Textile World,* Vol. 78 (1930), p. 659.

UNIT THREE

KING COTTON: ITS IMPORTANCE AND USE

"Cotton is king," the old slogan that indicated the supremacy of cotton exports in American trade, may well be applied to the relation of cotton to the fibers, for it is the most universally used of all fibers. There is, in fact, practically no cloth or article made of textile fibers for which cotton is not suitable.

Courtesy Bureau of Plant Industry, U. S. D. A.
FIG. 114.—Cotton plant with opened bolls.

Seventy-two per cent of all the raw fibers produced in the world are cotton. This fiber makes up the bulk of the clothing and household fabrics and has a wide range of use in the industries; for example, in automobile tires and aircraft fabrics. In the United States, approximately one-third of the cotton goes into clothing, one-third into industry, and one-third into articles for household use. The several vegetable fibers of more or less importance in the textile industries are classified according to the part of the plant in which they are found, as seed hairs, bast, and stem fibers. Cotton is the seed

177

纤维化学

著者：海野正
出版者：东京大阪三省堂
出版时间：1936 年
历史馆藏：南通学院

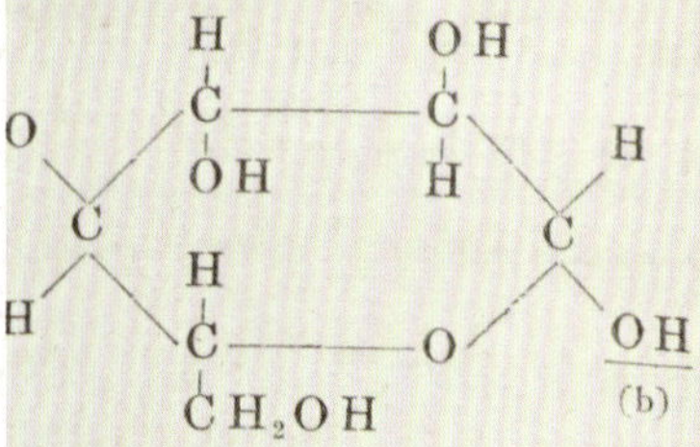

化　　學

型葡萄糖の構造式

はあるが，その大約を示せば多數の
-H と (b) の -OH との間にグリ
うに長鎖狀に連なつて纖維素分子を
の X 線的研究，階段的に起る纖維
イド性等によつても支持される．

植 物 纖

大體に於て 100 內外と見るが至當
500 Å，幅 5 Å であると考へられる
かゝる式を纖維素に與ふることに
とが出來る．纖維素の分子は一端
端には半アセタール性の -OH 基
あるに非常に大きな纖維素の分子
であるから，その表れが甚だ小さ
によつて纖維素分子が漸ゝ小さく
維素が加水分解によつてセロビオ
に對しアルコール性の -OH 基
維素及びその誘導體が粘度の大な

Rayon Warp Preparation and Quilling

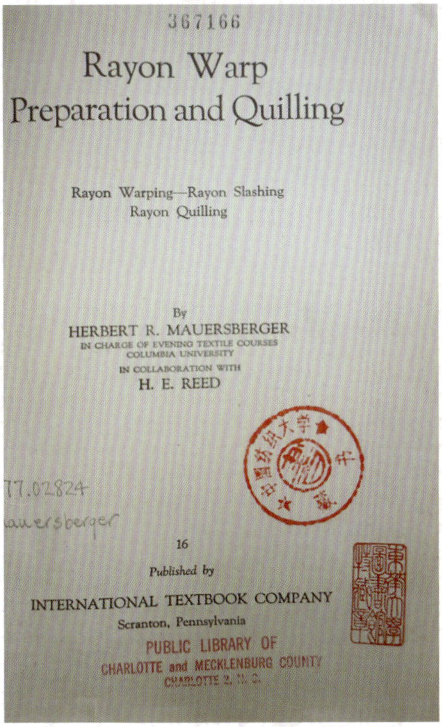
367166

Rayon Warp
Preparation and Quilling

Rayon Warping—Rayon Slashing
Rayon Quilling

By
HERBERT R. MAUERSBERGER
IN CHARGE OF EVENING TEXTILE COURSES
COLUMBIA UNIVERSITY
IN COLLABORATION WITH
H. E. REED

16

Published by
INTERNATIONAL TEXTBOOK COMPANY
Scranton, Pennsylvania

著者：HERBERT R.MAUERSBERGER
出版者：INTERNATIONAL TEXTBOOK COMPANY
出版时间：1943 年
历史馆藏：PUBLIC LIBRARY OF CHARLOTTE AND MECKLENBURG COUNTY

黏胶人造丝制造法

著者：D.L.Pellatt
出版者：商务印书馆
出版时间：1948 年
历史馆藏：苏南工专、南通学院

纤维工业辞典

著者：黄希阁
出版者：中国纺织染工程研究所
出版时间：1948 年
历史馆藏：苏南工专、私立中国纺织工学院

Worsted Drawing and Spinning Calculations

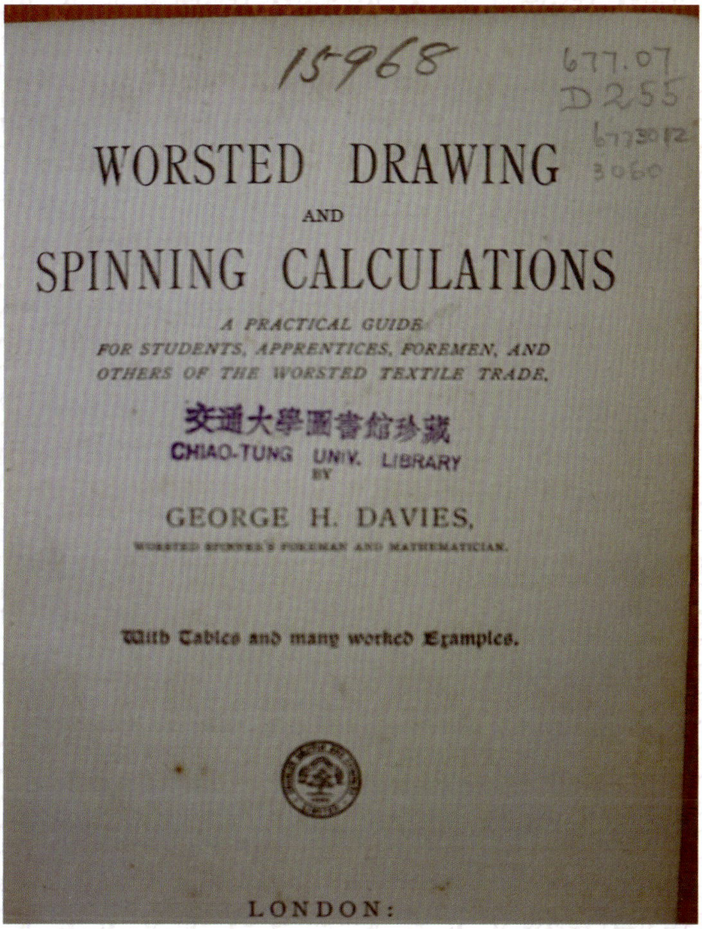

WORSTED DRAWING

AND

SPINNING CALCULATIONS

A PRACTICAL GUIDE
FOR STUDENTS, APPRENTICES, FOREMEN, AND OTHERS OF THE WORSTED TEXTILE TRADE.

BY

GEORGE H. DAVIES,

WORSTED SPINNER'S FOREMAN AND MATHEMATICIAN.

With Tables and many worked Examples.

LONDON:

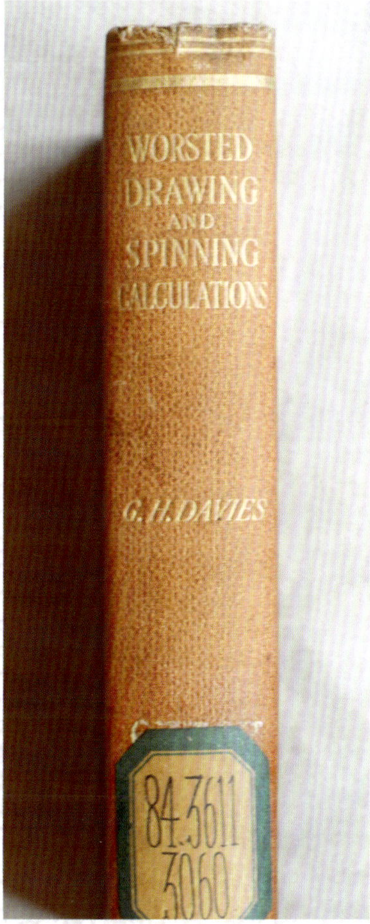

著者：George.H. Davies.
出版者：Charles Griffin & Company. Ltd.
出版时间：1923 年　　　　历史馆藏：交通大学

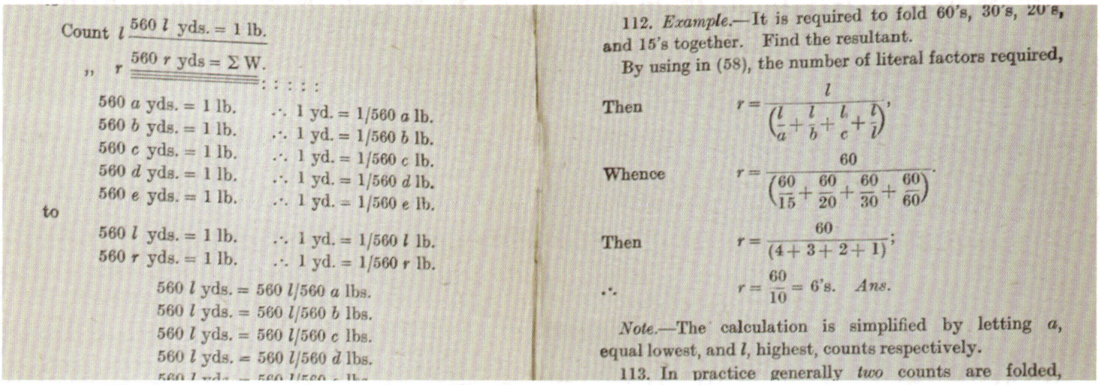

Count l $\dfrac{560\ l \text{ yds.} = 1 \text{ lb.}}{}$

,, r $560\ r$ yds $= \Sigma$ W.

$560\ a$ yds. = 1 lb.	∴ 1 yd. = $1/560\ a$ lb.
$560\ b$ yds. = 1 lb.	∴ 1 yd. = $1/560\ b$ lb.
$560\ c$ yds. = 1 lb.	∴ 1 yd. = $1/560\ c$ lb.
$560\ d$ yds. = 1 lb.	∴ 1 yd. = $1/560\ d$ lb.
$560\ e$ yds. = 1 lb.	∴ 1 yd. = $1/560\ e$ lb.

to

$560\ l$ yds. = 1 lb.	∴ 1 yd. = $1/560\ l$ lb.
$560\ r$ yds. = 1 lb.	∴ 1 yd. = $1/560\ r$ lb.

$560\ l$ yds. = $560\ l/560\ a$ lbs.
$560\ l$ yds. = $560\ l/560\ b$ lbs.
$560\ l$ yds. = $560\ l/560\ c$ lbs.
$560\ l$ yds. = $560\ l/560\ d$ lbs.

112. *Example.*—It is required to fold 60's, 30's, 20's, and 15's together. Find the resultant.

By using in (58), the number of literal factors required,

Then $$r = \frac{l}{\left(\frac{l}{a}+\frac{l}{b}+\frac{l}{c}+\frac{l}{l}\right)},$$

Whence $$r = \frac{60}{\left(\frac{60}{15}+\frac{60}{20}+\frac{60}{30}+\frac{60}{60}\right)}.$$

Then $$r = \frac{60}{(4+3+2+1)};$$

∴ $$r = \frac{60}{10} = 6\text{'s}. \quad \textit{Ans.}$$

Note.—The calculation is simplified by letting a, equal lowest, and l, highest, counts respectively.

113. In practice generally *two* counts are folded,

纺纱学

编者：成希文
出版者：商务印书馆
出版时间：1939 年
历史馆藏：国营上海毛麻纺织公司

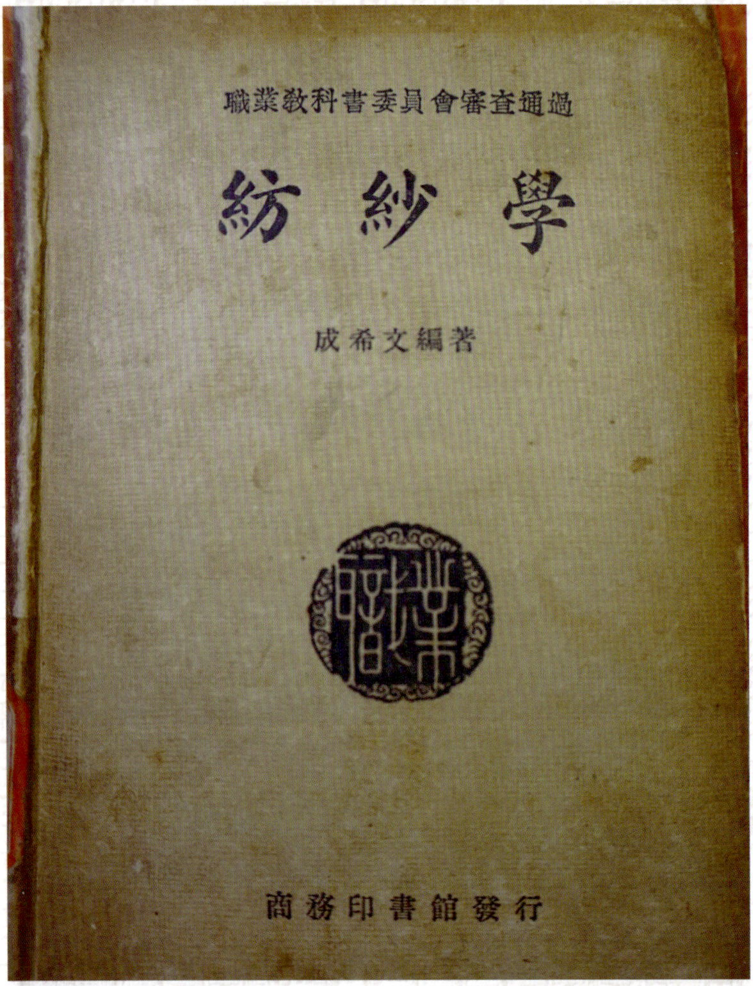

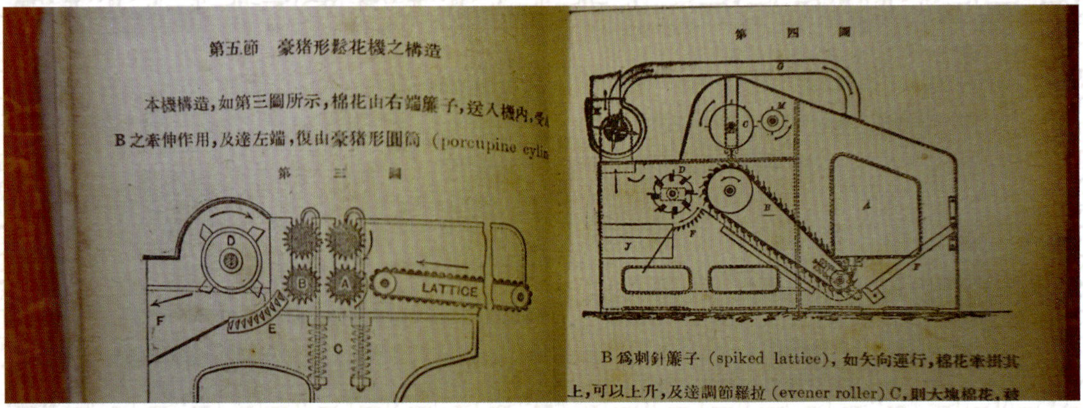
第五節 毫猪形鬆花機之構造

本機構造，如第三圖所示，棉花由右端簾子，送入機內，受
B之牽伸作用，及達左端，復由毫猪形圓筒（porcupine cylin

第三圖

第四圖

B爲刺針簾子（spiked lattice），如矢向運行，棉花牽掛其
上，可以上升，及達調節羅拉（evener roller）C，則大塊棉花，被

最新纺纱计算学（上、下卷）

著者：何达
出版者：三省堂
出版时间：1945 年
历史馆藏：苏南工专、上海高级纺织技工学校、中国纤维工业研究所

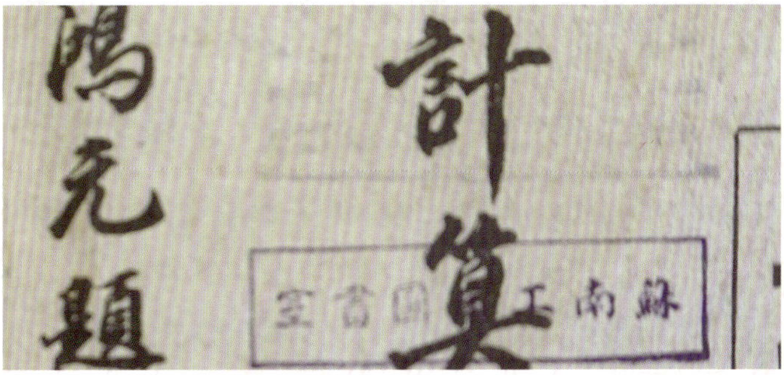

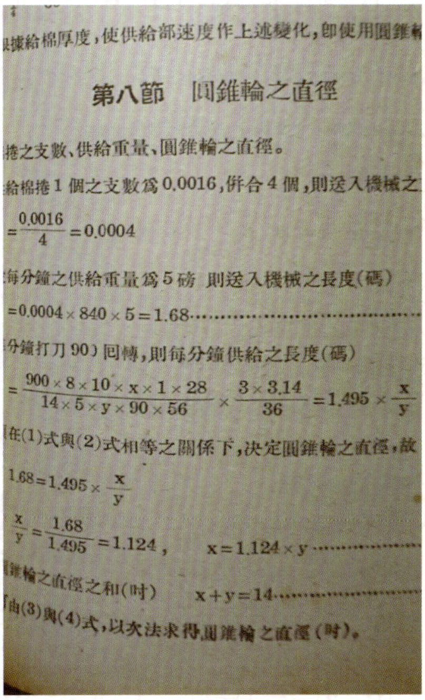

據給棉厚度，使供給部速度作上述變化，即使用圓錐輪

第八節　圓錐輪之直徑

捲之支數、供給重量、圓錐輪之直徑。

給棉捲 1 個之支數爲 0.0016，倂合 4 個，則送入機械之

$= \frac{0.0016}{4} = 0.0004$

每分鐘之供給重量爲 5 磅　則送入機械之長度(碼)

$= 0.0004 \times 840 \times 5 = 1.68 \cdots\cdots$

分鐘打刀 90) 回轉，則每分鐘供給之長度(碼)

$= \frac{900 \times 8 \times 10 \times x \times 1 \times 28}{14 \times 5 \times y \times 90 \times 56} \times \frac{3 \times 3.14}{36} = 1.495 \times \frac{x}{y}$

在(1)式與(2)式相等之關係下，決定圓錐輪之直徑，故

$1.68 = 1.495 \times \frac{x}{y}$

$\frac{x}{y} = \frac{1.68}{1.495} = 1.124$，　$x = 1.124 \times y \cdots\cdots$

錐輪之直徑之和(吋)　$x + y = 14 \cdots\cdots$

由(3)與(4)式，以次法求得圓錐輪之直徑(吋)。

纺绩工程学

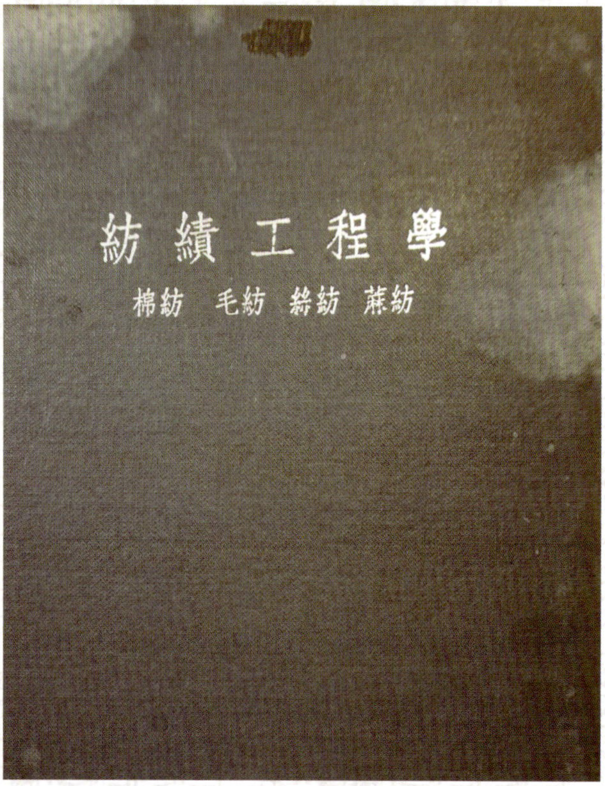

编者：黄希阁
出版者：中国纺织染工程研究所
出版时间：1947 年
历史馆藏：南通学院、上海纺织工业学校

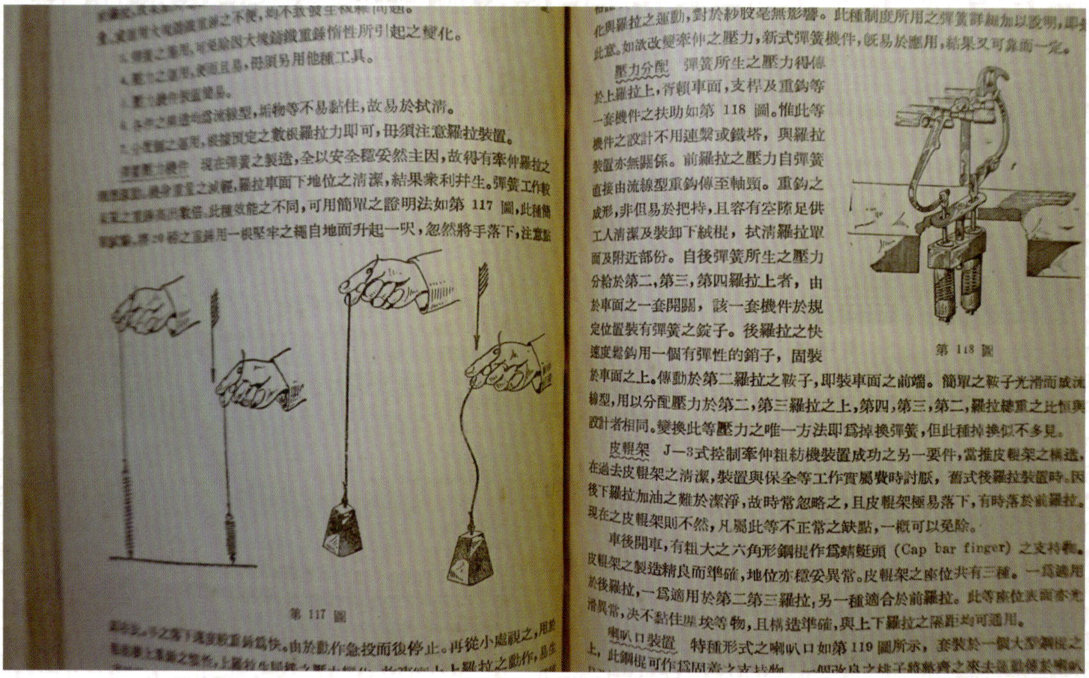

[illegible]起之變化。
[illegible]毋須另用他種工具。
[illegible]垢物等不易黏住，故易於拭淸。
[illegible]即可，毋須注意羅拉裝置。
[illegible] 現在彈簧之製造，全以安全穩妥爲主因，故得有牽伸羅拉之[illegible]羅拉車面下地位之淸潔，結果衆利幷生。彈簧工作較[illegible]此種效能之不同，可用簡單之證明法如第 117 圖，此種[illegible]用一根堅牢之繩自地面升起一呎，忽然將手落下，注意[illegible]

第 117 圖

[illegible]化與羅拉之運動，對於紗股毫無影響。此種制度所用之彈簧詳細加以說明，[illegible]此意。如欲改變牽伸之壓力，新式彈簧機件，旣易於應用，結果又可劃一。

壓力分配 彈簧所生之壓力得傳於上羅拉上，背賴車面，支桿及重鈎等一套機件之扶助如第 118 圖。惟此等機件之設計不用連繫或鐵塔，與羅拉裝置亦無關係。前羅拉之壓力自彈簧直接由流線型重鈎傳至軸頸。重鈎之成形，非但易於把持，且容有空隙足供工人淸潔及裝卸下絨棍，拭淸羅拉單面及附近部份。自後彈簧所生之壓力分給於第二，第三，第四羅拉上者，由於車面之一套開關，該一套機件於規定位置裝有彈簧之錠子。後羅拉之快速度鬆鈎用一個有彈性的銷子，固裝於車面之上。傳動於第二羅拉之鞍子，即裝車面之前端。簡單之鞍子光滑而成流線型，用以分配壓力於第二，第三羅拉之上，第四，第三，第二，羅拉總重之比恒與設計者相同。變換此等壓力之唯一方法即爲掉換彈簧，但此種掉換似不多見。

第 118 圖

皮輥架 J—3式控制牽伸粗紡機裝置成功之另一要件，當推皮輥架之構造，在過去皮輥架之淸潔，裝置與保全等工作實屬費時討厭，舊式後羅拉裝置時，因後下羅拉加油之難於潔淨，故時常忽略之，且皮輥架極易落下，有時落於前羅拉。現在之皮輥架則不然，凡屬此等不正常之缺點，一槪可以免除。

車後開車，有粗大之六角形鋼棍作爲蜻蜓頭 (Cap bar finger) 之支持物。皮輥架之製造精良而準確，地位亦穩妥異常。皮輥架之座位共有三種。一爲適用於後羅拉，一爲適用於第二第三羅拉，另一種適合於前羅拉。此等座位表面亦光滑異常，決不黏住塵埃等物，且構造準確，與上下羅拉之隔距均可適用。

喇叭口裝置 特種形式之喇叭口如第 119 圖所示，套裝於一個大型鋼棍之上，此鋼棍可作爲固着之支持物。[illegible]

Analysis of Woven Fabrics

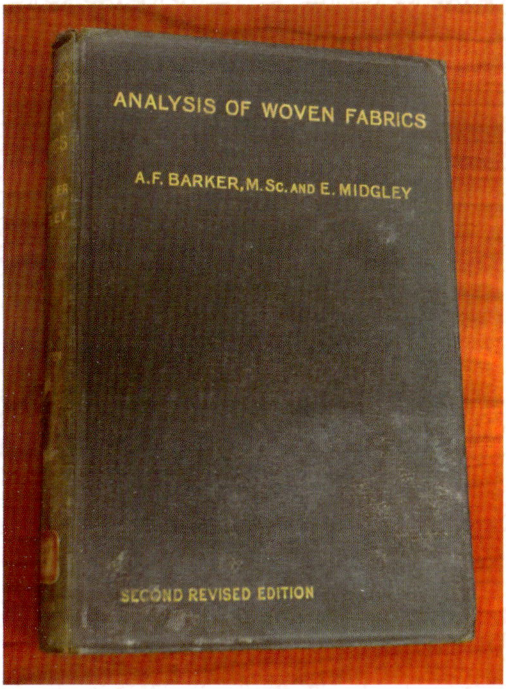

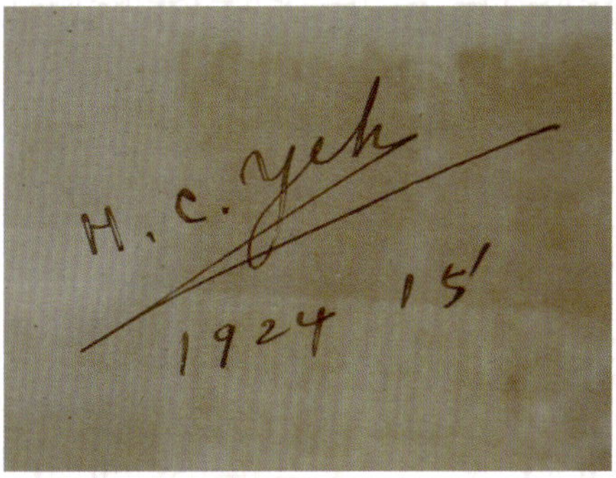

著者：A. F. Barker, E. Midgley
出版者：Scott, Greenwood & Son
出版时间：1922 年
历史馆藏：校友捐赠

Foot-power Loom Weaving

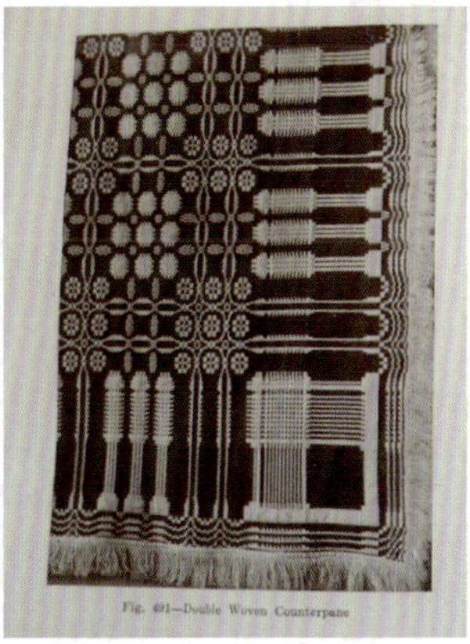

著者：Edward F. Worst　出版者：The Bruce Publishing Company
出版时间：1924 年　历史馆藏：南通学院

Hand-loom Weaving

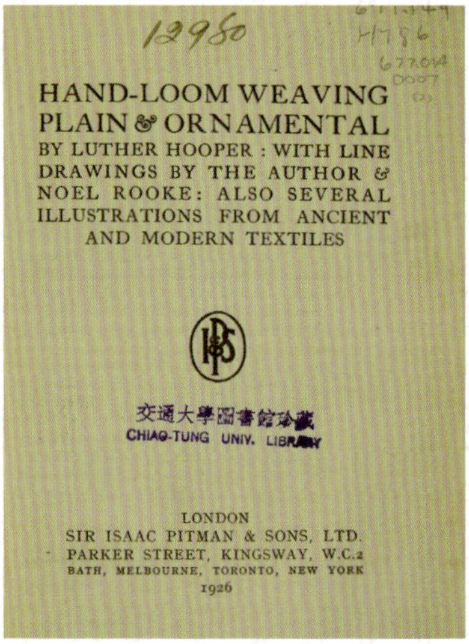
12980

HAND-LOOM WEAVING
PLAIN & ORNAMENTAL
BY LUTHER HOOPER : WITH LINE DRAWINGS BY THE AUTHOR & NOEL ROOKE: ALSO SEVERAL ILLUSTRATIONS FROM ANCIENT AND MODERN TEXTILES

LONDON
SIR ISAAC PITMAN & SONS, LTD.
PARKER STREET, KINGSWAY, W.C.2
BATH, MELBOURNE, TORONTO, NEW YORK
1926

著者：Luther Hooper
出版者：Sir Isaac Pitman & Sons, Ltd.
出版时间：1926 年
历史馆藏：交通大学

织物构造

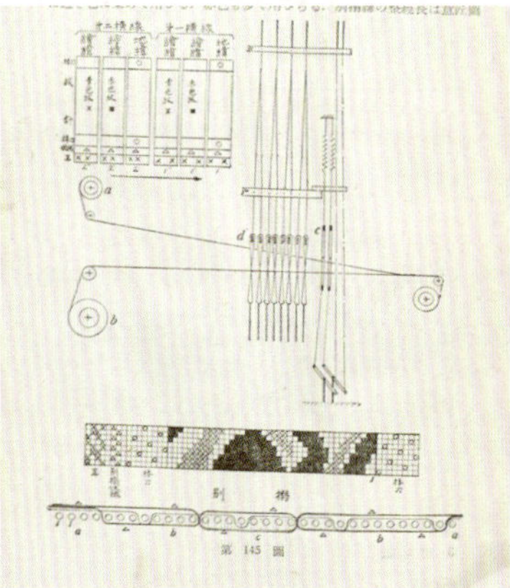

著者：太田勤治
出版者：东京大阪三省堂
出版时间：1926 年

机织法（上、下）

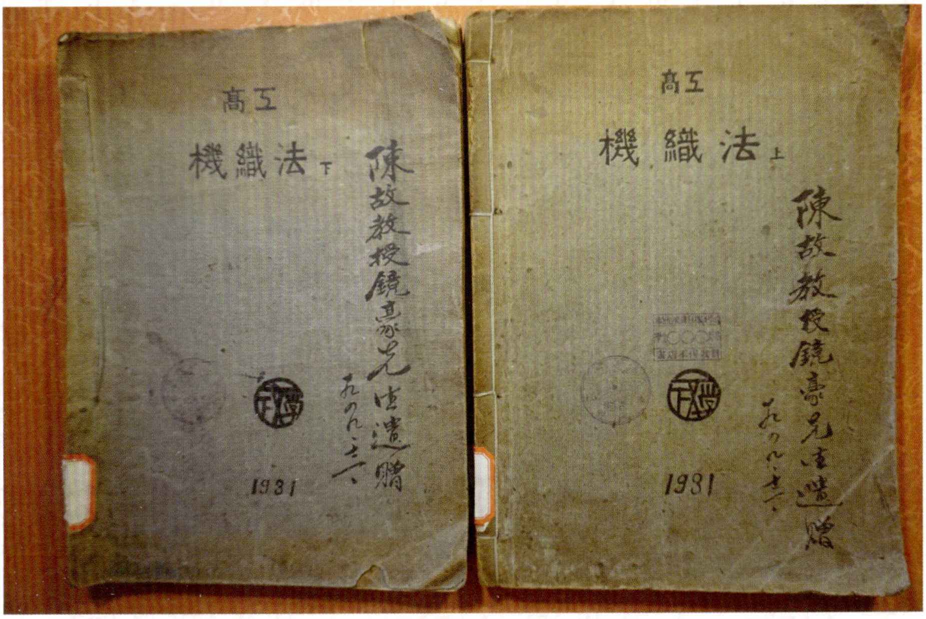

著者：吴子展　　出版时间：1931 年，手写线装
历史馆藏：南通学院、湖南省立高级工科职业学校

Simple Weaving

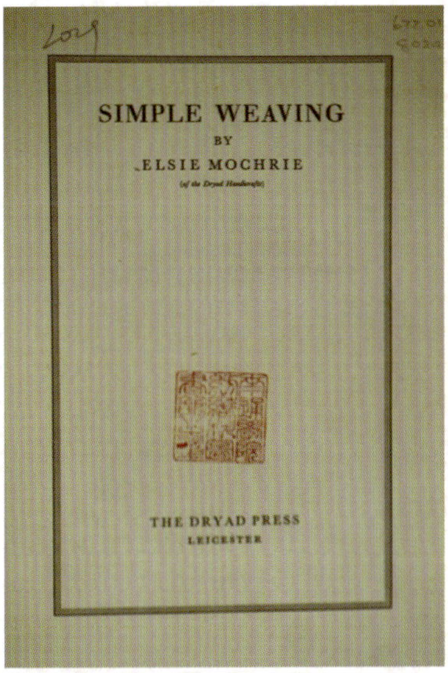

著者：Elsie Mochrie
出版者：The Dryad Press
出版时间：1934 年
历史馆藏：南通学院

实用机织法纹地组织

著者：张元寿（兼发行）
出版时间：1934 年，宣纸线装
历史馆藏：南通学院

实用织物组合学

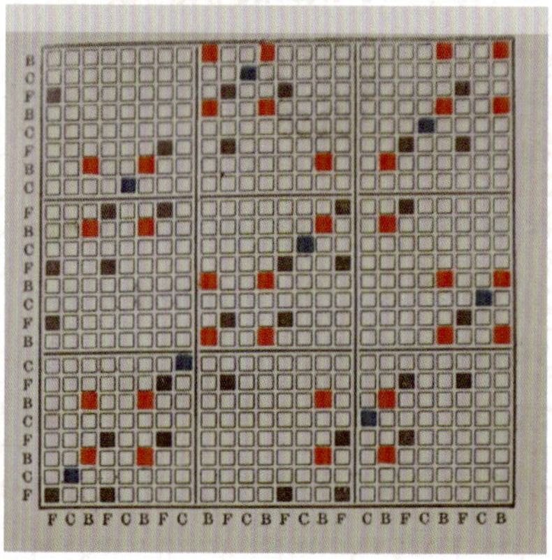

著者：蒋乃镛
出版者：商务印书馆
出版时间：1936 年
历史馆藏：私立上海纺织工业专科学校

Textile Design and Colour

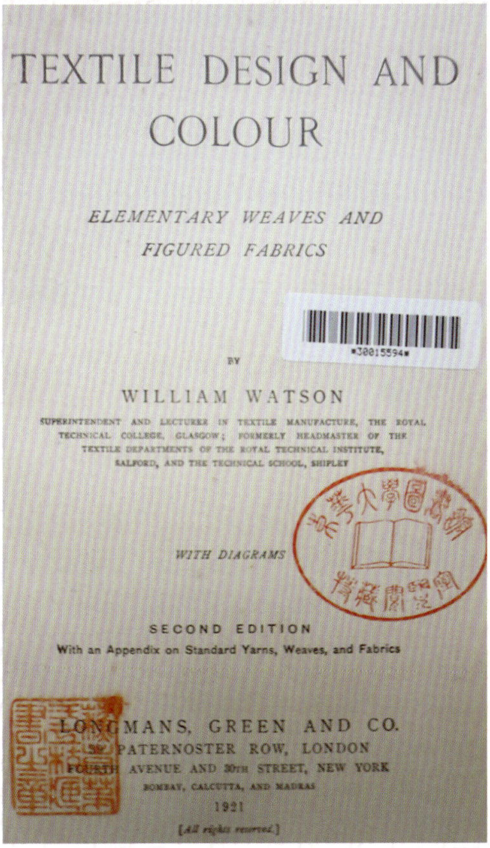

TEXTILE DESIGN AND COLOUR

ELEMENTARY WEAVES AND FIGURED FABRICS

BY

WILLIAM WATSON

SUPERINTENDENT AND LECTURER IN TEXTILE MANUFACTURE, THE ROYAL TECHNICAL COLLEGE, GLASGOW; FORMERLY HEADMASTER OF THE TEXTILE DEPARTMENTS OF THE ROYAL TECHNICAL INSTITUTE, SALFORD, AND THE TECHNICAL SCHOOL, SHIPLEY

WITH DIAGRAMS

SECOND EDITION

With an Appendix on Standard Yarns, Weaves, and Fabrics

LONGMANS, GREEN AND CO.

39 PATERNOSTER ROW, LONDON

FOURTH AVENUE AND 30TH STREET, NEW YORK

BOMBAY, CALCUTTA, AND MADRAS

1921

[*All rights reserved.*]

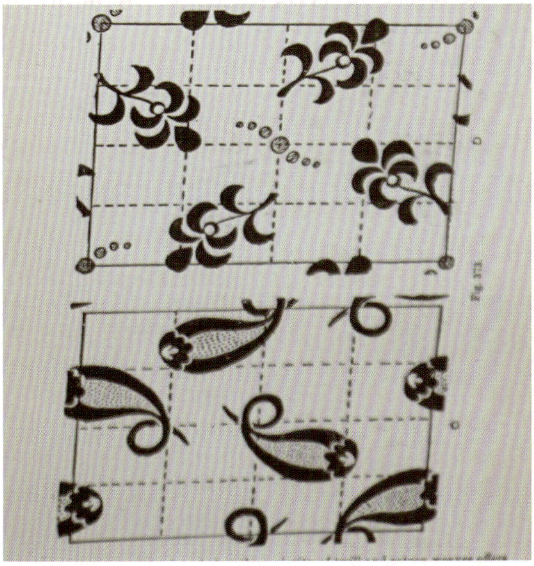

著者：W. WATSON

出版者：LONGMANS,GREEN AND CO. LTD.

出版时间：1921 年

历史馆藏：苏州工业学校纺织染学会、

苏南工专、南通学院、

天津鸿雪印书社驻申办事处

实用色染学

著者：中岛武太郎
出版者：东京丸善株式会社
出版时间：1931 年

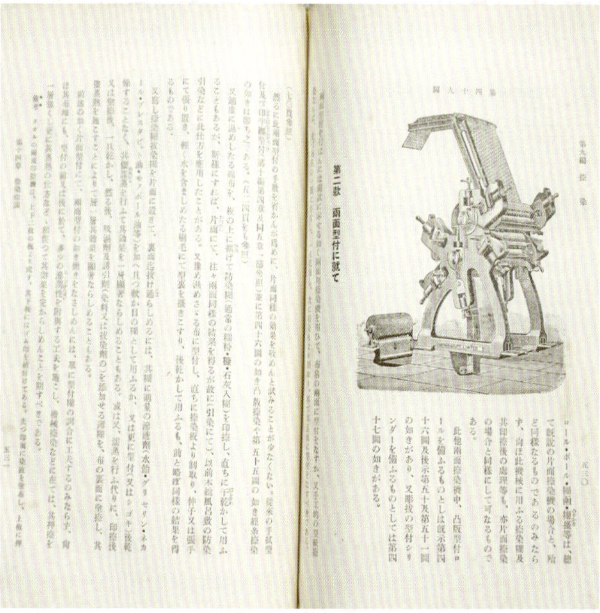

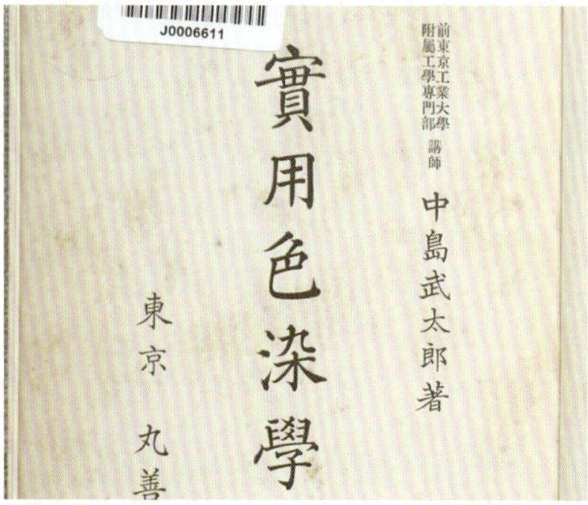

矿物颜料

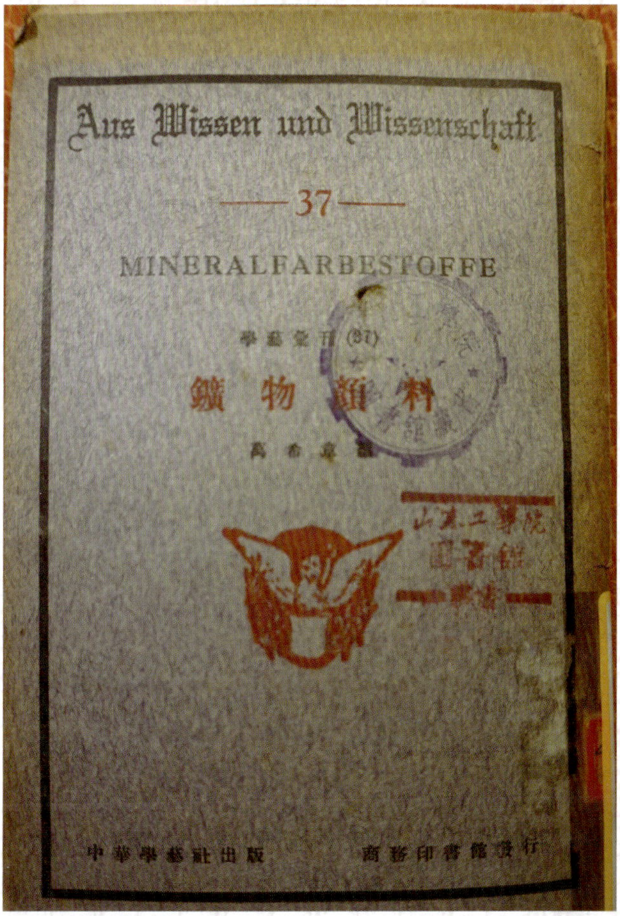

著者：万希章
出版者：中华学艺社
出版时间：1935 年
历史馆藏：山东工学院、山东省立工业专科学校、青岛工学院

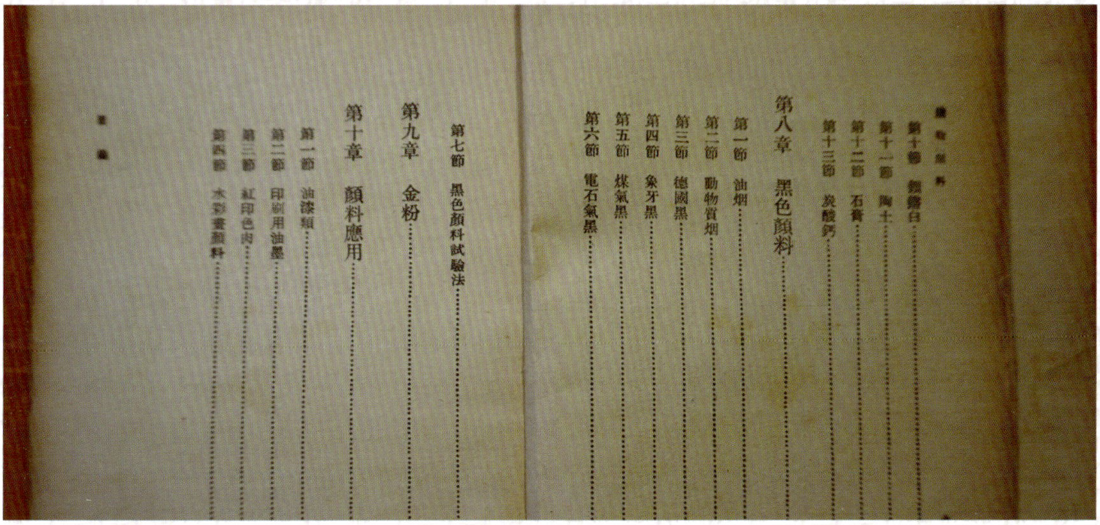

染织物整理

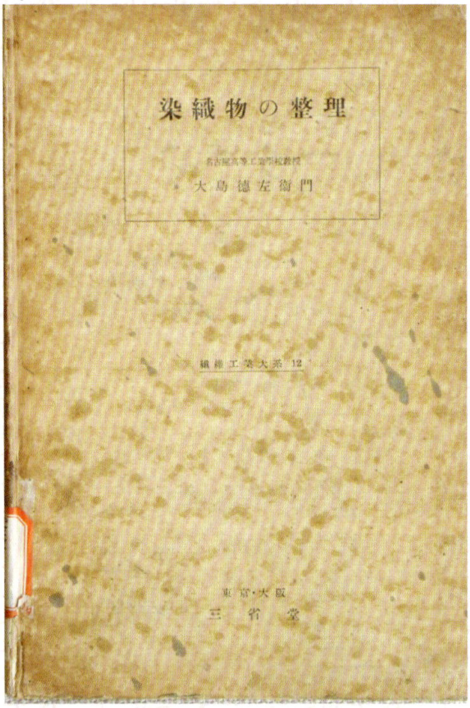

著者：大岛德左卫门
出版者：东京大阪三省堂
出版时间：1936 年
历史馆藏：中国纺织染工程研究所

染色纹样史研究

著者：明石染人
出版者：东京万里阁书房
出版时间：1944 年
历史馆藏：南通学院

Carpet Manufacture

编者：Fred Bradbury
出版者：LANGDALE HOUSE, OR MUNICIPAL TECHNICAL INSTITUTE,BELFAST
出版时间：1904 年
历史馆藏：交通大学

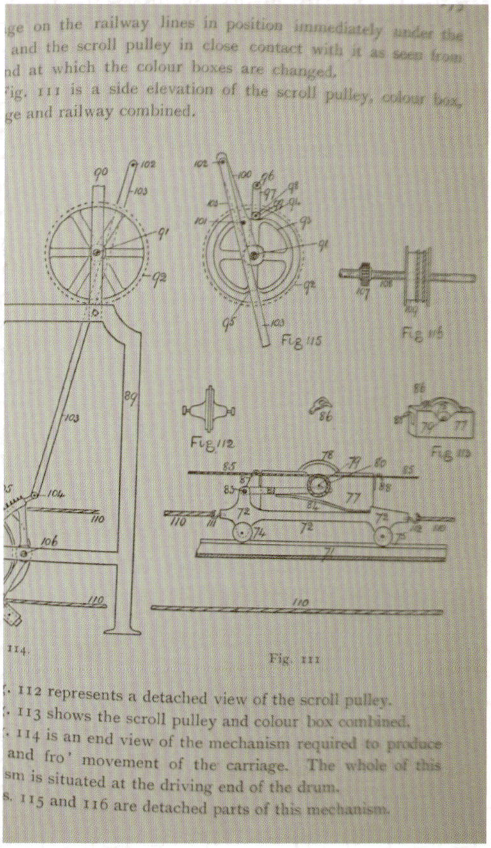

ge on the railway lines in position immediately under the
and the scroll pulley in close contact with it as seen from
nd at which the colour boxes are changed.
ig. 111 is a side elevation of the scroll pulley, colour box,
ge and railway combined.

114.

Fig. 111

. 112 represents a detached view of the scroll pulley.
. 113 shows the scroll pulley and colour box combined.
. 114 is an end view of the mechanism required to produce
and fro' movement of the carriage. The whole of this
sm is situated at the driving end of the drum.
s. 115 and 116 are detached parts of this mechanism.

AXMINSTER CARPETS. 213

the tappet or cam shaft 22, as seen from the back of the loom. This shaft is the most important piece of mechanism in the loom since from it nearly all the varied and compound motions are

Fig. 147.

obtained. The numbers on this illustration refer to similar parts described in connection with Figs. 159 and 160.

It is proposed to describe the Axminster Carpet Loom and the

The Textile Industry

著者：WILLIAM S.MURPHY　出版者：The Gresham.Pubishing Company
出版时间：1912 年　历史馆藏：南通学院

Winding, Warping and Weaving Machinery

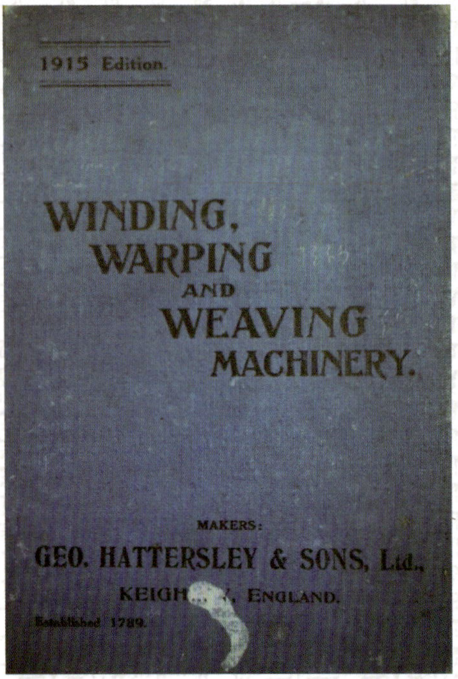

出版者：Geo. Hattersley & Sons, Ltd.
出版时间：1915 年
历史馆藏：诚孚纺织专科学校

Textiles

著者：A. F. Barker
出版者：D. Van Nostrand Company
出版时间：1919 年
历史馆藏：GIT

Textiles

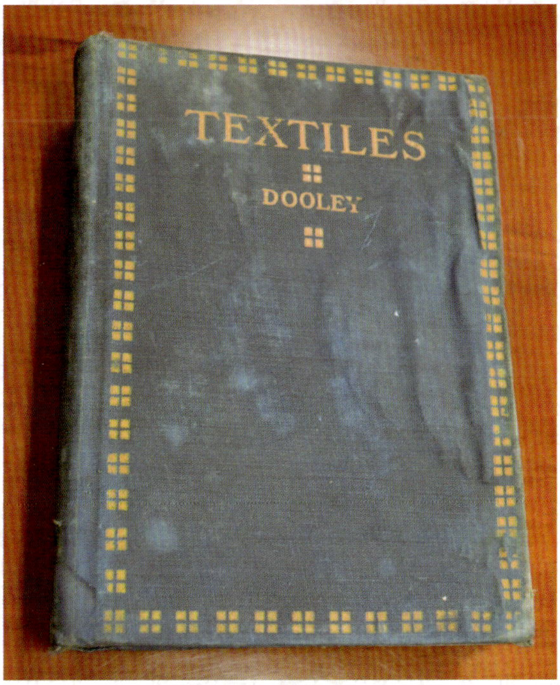

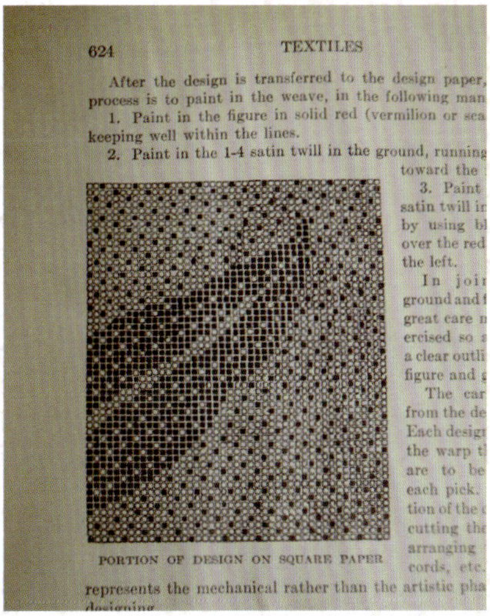

624 TEXTILES

After the design is transferred to the design paper,
process is to paint in the weave, in the following man
1. Paint in the figure in solid red (vermilion or sca
keeping well within the lines.
2. Paint in the 1-4 satin twill in the ground, running
toward the
3. Paint
satin twill ir
by using bl
over the red
the left.
In joi
ground and t
great care n
ercised so
a clear outli
figure and g
The car
from the de
Each design
the warp t
are to be
each pick.
tion of the
cutting th
arranging
cords, etc.

PORTION OF DESIGN ON SQUARE PAPER

represents the mechanical rather than the artistic pha

著者：William H. Dooley
出版者：D. C. Heath and Company
出版时间：1924 年
历史馆藏：南通学院

Ornamental Design for Woven Fabrics

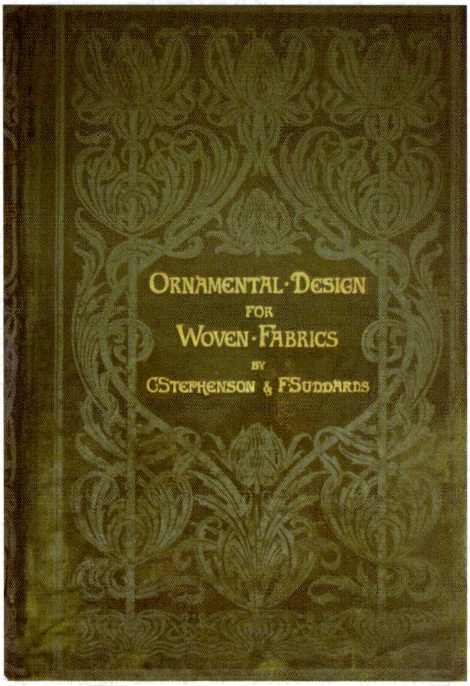

A TEXT BOOK DEALING WITH
ORNAMENTAL DESIGN
FOR
WOVEN FABRICS
BY
C. STEPHENSON AND F. SUDDARDS
交通大學圖書館珍藏
CHIAO-TUNG UNIV. LIBRARY
FOURTH EDITION
METHUEN & CO. LTD.
36 ESSEX STREET W.C.
LONDON

著者：C. Stephenson, F. Suddards
出版者：Methuen & Co. Ltd.
出版时间：1924 年
历史馆藏：交通大学

Advanced Textile Design

ADVANCED
TEXTILE DESIGN
BY
WILLIAM WATSON
30007930
SECOND EDITION
LONGMANS, GREEN AND CO.

著者：William Watson
出版者：Congmans, Green and Co.
出版时间：1925 年
历史馆藏：交通大学

Dissecting and Calculating Silk and Rayon Fabrics

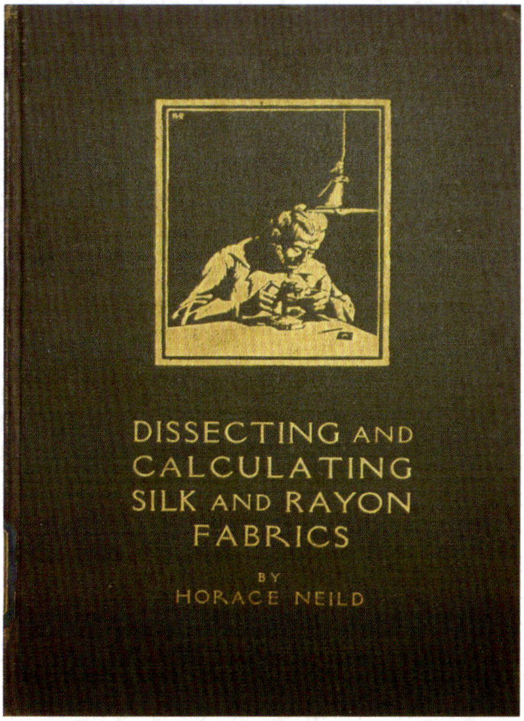

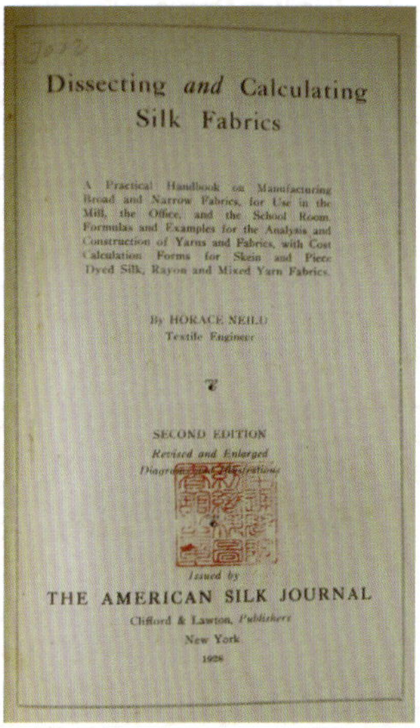

著者：Horace Neild
出版者：The American Silk Journal
出版时间：1928 年
历史馆藏：南通学院

Textile Recorder

著者：John Brooks　　出版者：HARLEQUIN Manchester
出版时间：1929 年起　　历史馆藏：南通学院

Manufacture of Men's Clothing

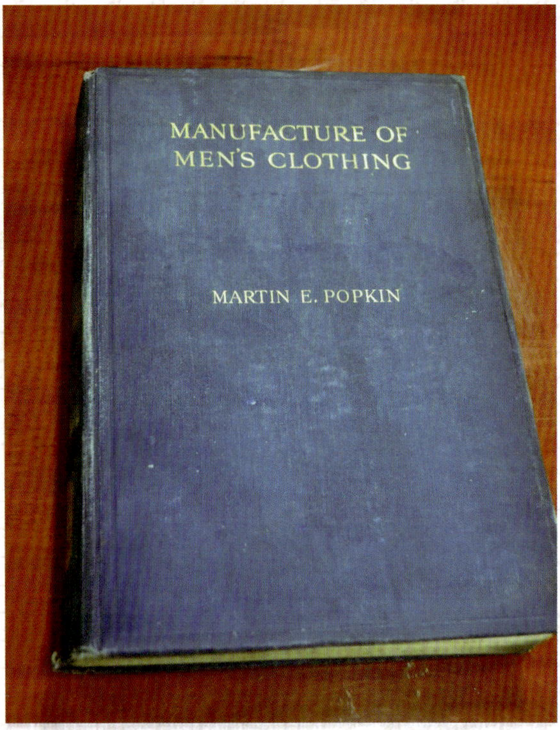

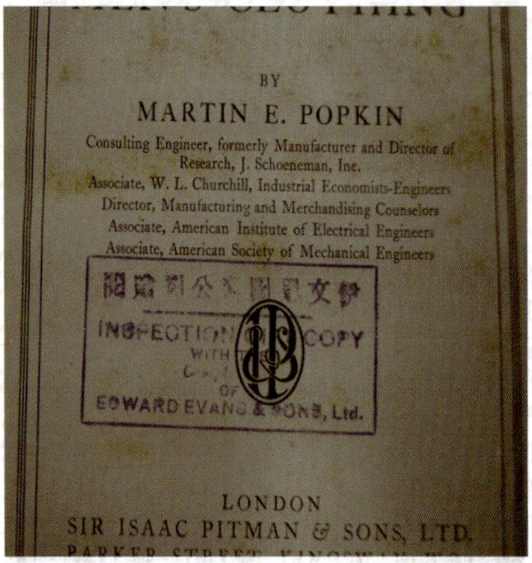

著者：Martin E. Popkin
出版者：Sir Isaac Pitman & Sons, Ltd.
出版时间：1929 年
历史馆藏：公司捐赠

Ornamentation and Textile Design

著者：Aldred F. Barker
出版者：Methuer & Co. Ltd.
出版时间：1930 年
历史馆藏：交通大学

Textiles on Test

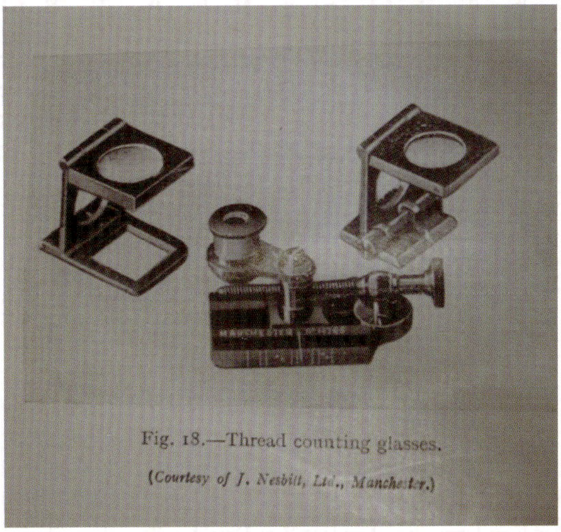

著者：J. Guilfoyle Williams
出版者：Chapman and Hall, Ltd.
出版时间：1931 年
历史馆藏：交通大学

The Textiles Student's Manual

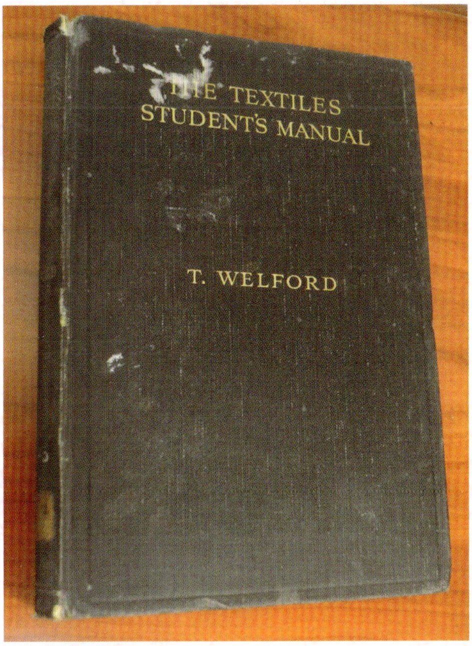

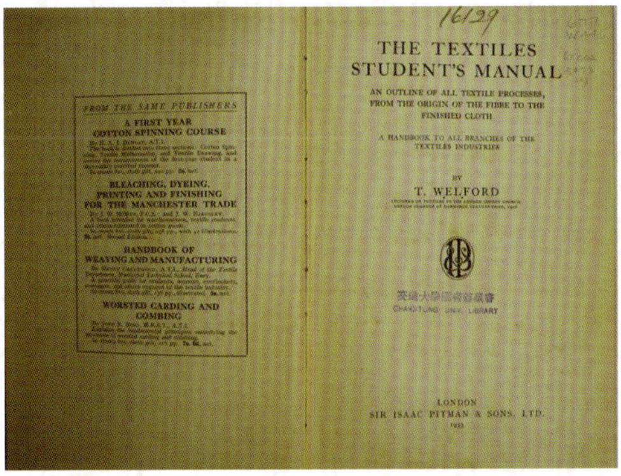

著者：T. Welford
出版者：Sir Isaac Pitman & Sons, Ltd.
出版时间：1933 年
历史馆藏：交通大学

British and Dominion Textile Industry

出版时间：1934 年
出版者：John Worrall Ltd.
历史馆藏：南通学院

纺织工学小丛书

著者：朱升芹等
出版者：商务印书馆　　出版时间：1935 年
历史馆藏：苏南工专、苏州工业学校、无锡庆丰纺织公司、华东纺织管理局干部学校、上海工业专科学校

纺织工厂管理学

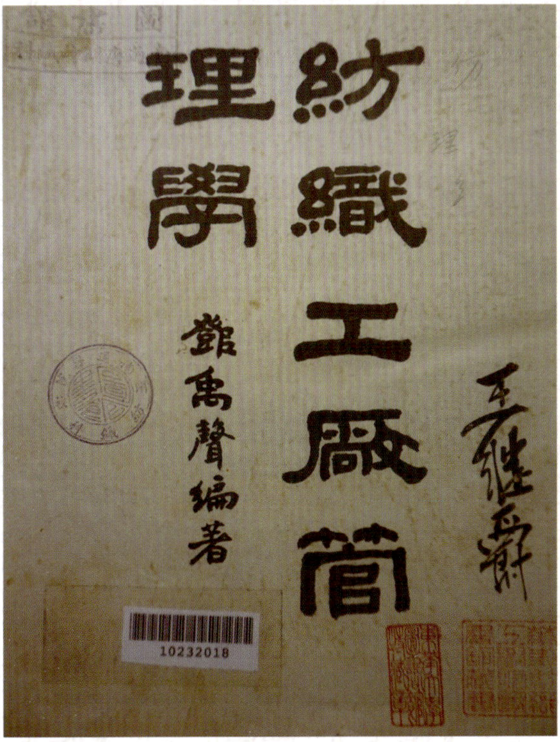

著者：邓禹声
出版者：南通学院纺织科学友会
出版时间：1936 年
历史馆藏：南通学院

实践纺织学

著者：广川治雄
出版者：工业图书株式会社
出版时间：1937 年
历史馆藏：南通学院

纤维防水防火加工法

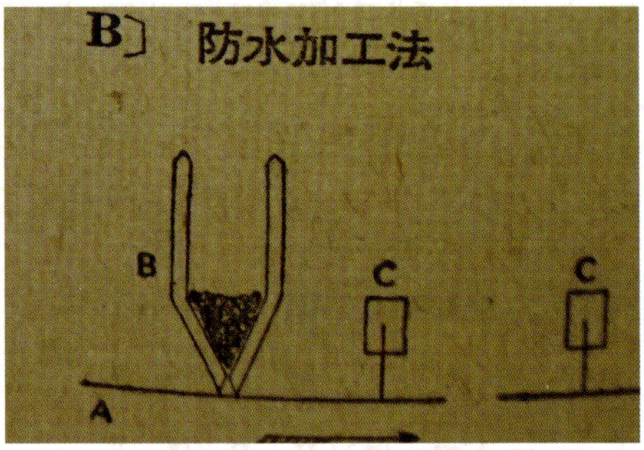

著者：熊田健一
出版者：修教社书院
出版时间：1938 年
历史馆藏：苏南工专

中国之纺织业及其出品

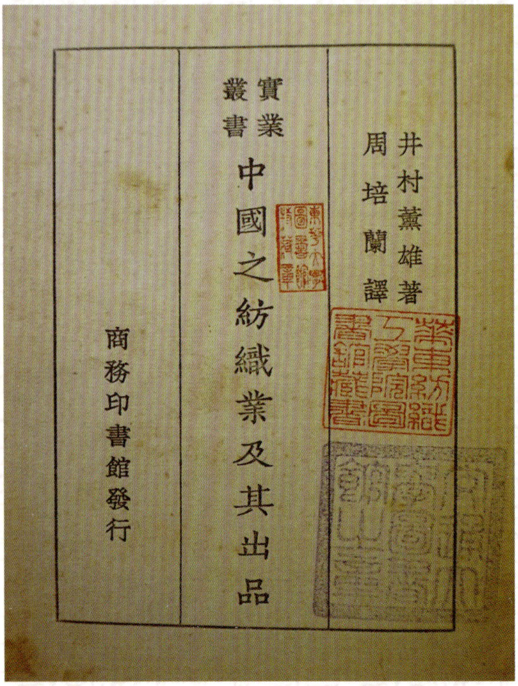

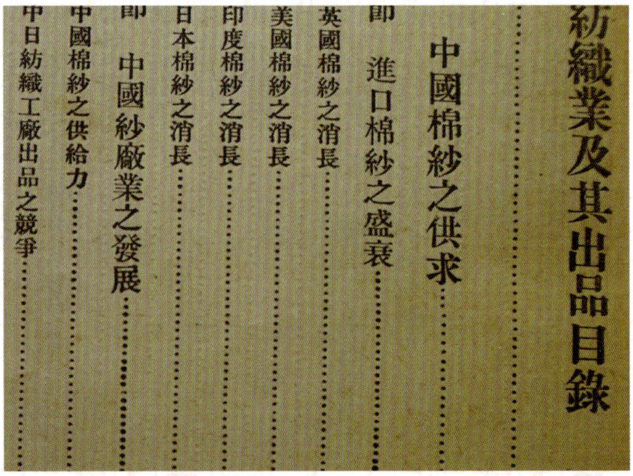

著者：井村薰雄
出版者：商务印书馆
出版时间：1939 年
历史馆藏：南通大学

Introduction to Textile Chemistry

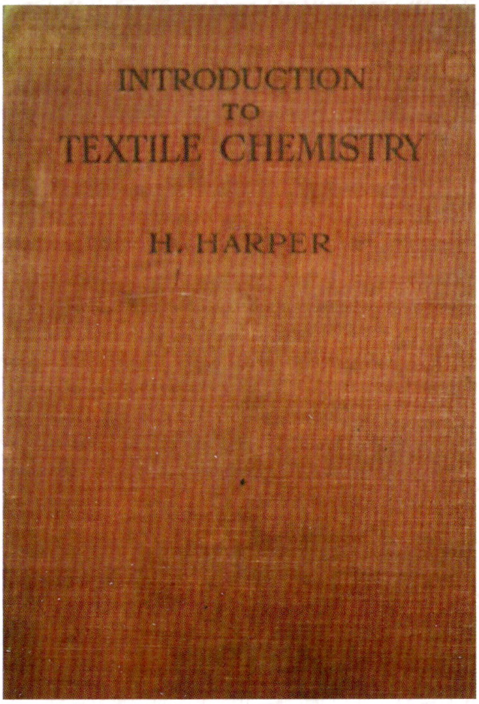

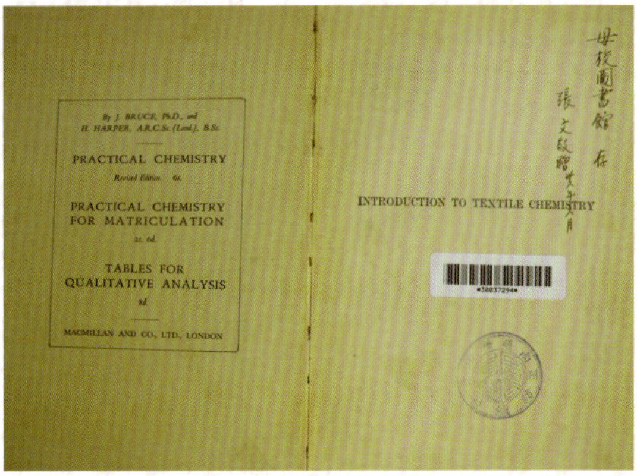

著者：H. Harper
出版者：MacMillan and Co., Ltd.
出版时间：1939 年
历史馆藏：南通学院

Davison's Textile Blue Book

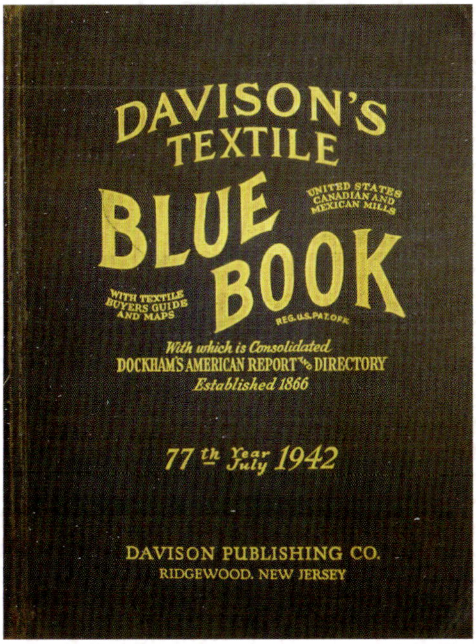

出版者：Davison Publishing Co.
出版时间：1942 年

Yarn and Cloth Calculation

BY
LLOYD H. JACKSON, M.S.
Cottonseed Delinting Company
Vernon, Texas
Formerly Associate Professor,
Department of Textile Engineering,
Texas Technological College, Lubbock, Texas
First Edition

著者：LLOYD H. JACKSON
出版者：TEXTTILE BOOK PUBLISHERS, INC.
出版时间：1946 年
历史馆藏：私立上海纺织工业学校

纺织日用手册

紡織日用手册
著作者
川沙 陸紹雲
日本東京高等工業學校紡織科
順昌紡織公司總經理
中國紡織染工程研究所出版

著者：陆绍云
出版者：中国纺织染工程研究所
出版时间：1946 年
历史馆藏：江苏省立工业专科学校

棉纺织工场之设计与管理

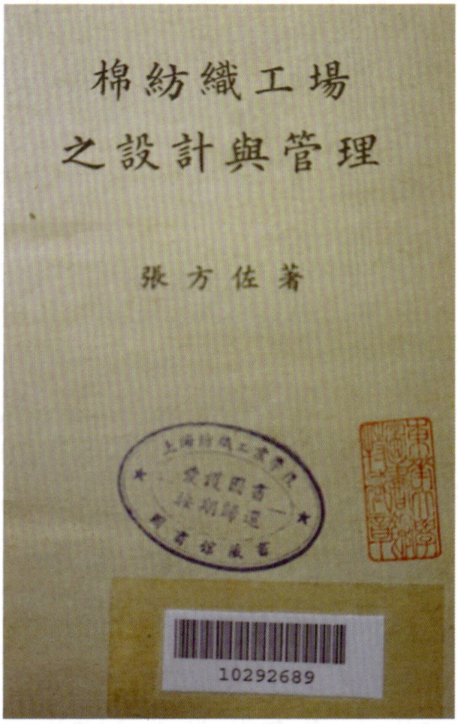

著者：张方佐
出版者：崇文印刷所
出版时间：1946 年
历史馆藏：上海纺织工业学校

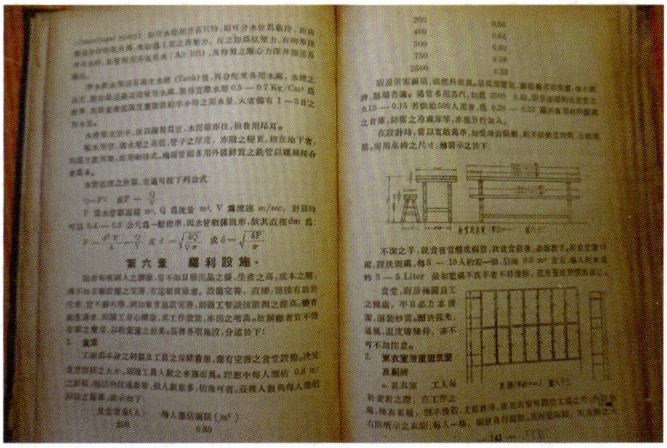

纺织工业

出版：商业月报社　　　　　出版时间：1947 年
历史馆藏：私立上海诚孚纺织专科学校、私立上海纺织工学院

America's Fabrics

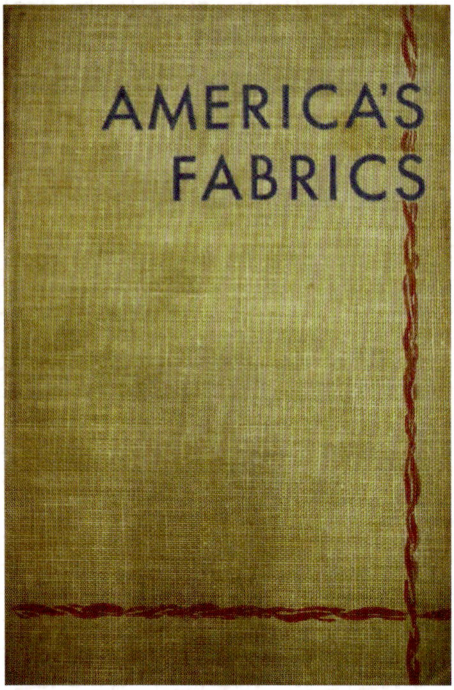

AMERICA'S FABRICS

Origin and History, Manufacture, Characteristics and Uses

ZELMA BENDURE · GLADYS PFEIFFER

Photographic Layout by Crystal Stephen

Fabric Photographs by Nat Messik

THE MACMILLAN COMPANY · NEW YORK · 1947

著者：Zelma Bendure, Gladys Pfeiffer
出版者：The MacMillan Company
出版时间：1947 年
历史馆藏：校友捐赠

私立上海纺织工业专科学校一览

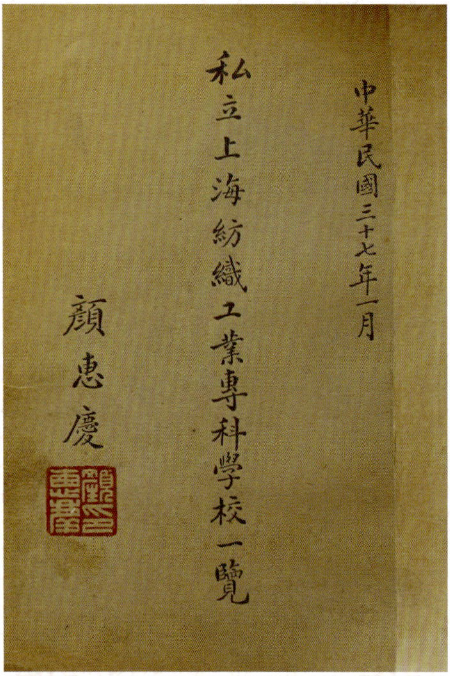
私立上海紡織工業專科學校一覽

中華民國三十七年一月

顏惠慶

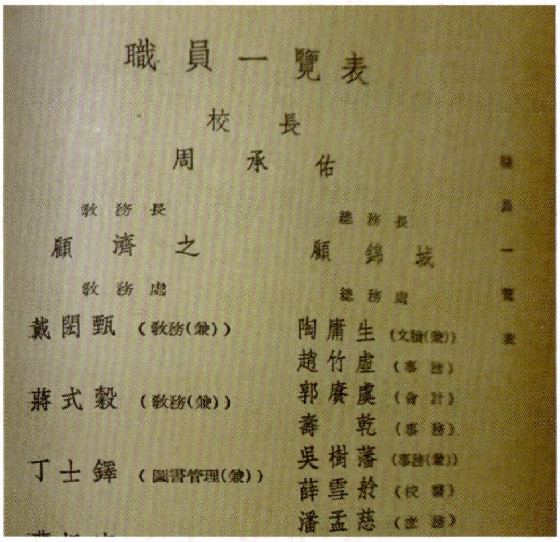
職員一覽表

校長

周承佑

教務長

顧濟之

教務處

戴閎甄（教務(兼)）

蔣式穀（教務(兼)）

丁士鐸（圖書管理(兼)）

總務長

顧錦坡

總務處

陶庸生

趙竹盧（事務）

郭賡虞（會計）

壽　乾（事務）

吳樹藩

薛雪舲

潘孟慈

著者：颜惠庆
时间：1948 年
内部资料未正式出版

纺织年刊

出版者：中国纺织学会
发行时间：1931-1935 年

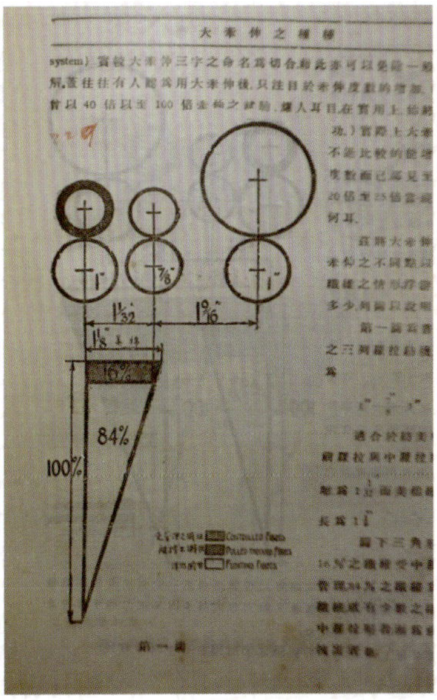

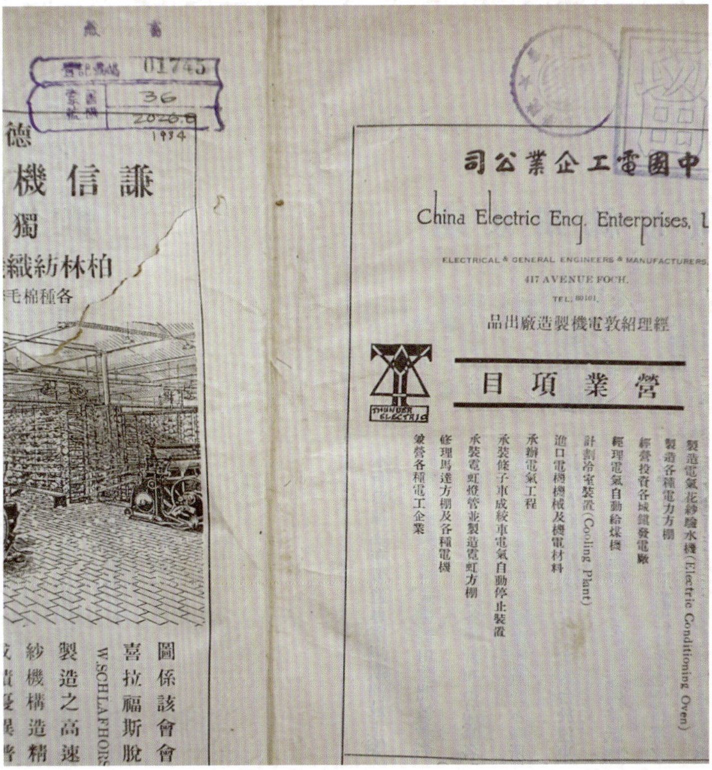

纺织周刊

出版者：纺织周刊社

发行时间：1931 年创刊，1931 年 -1935 年，1946 年 -1948 年连续出版

历史馆藏：南通学院、上海纺织工业学校、中国纺织染工程研究所

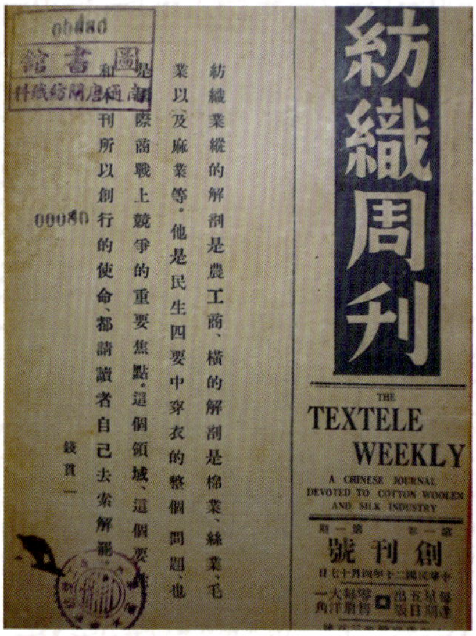

The Journal of the Textile Institute

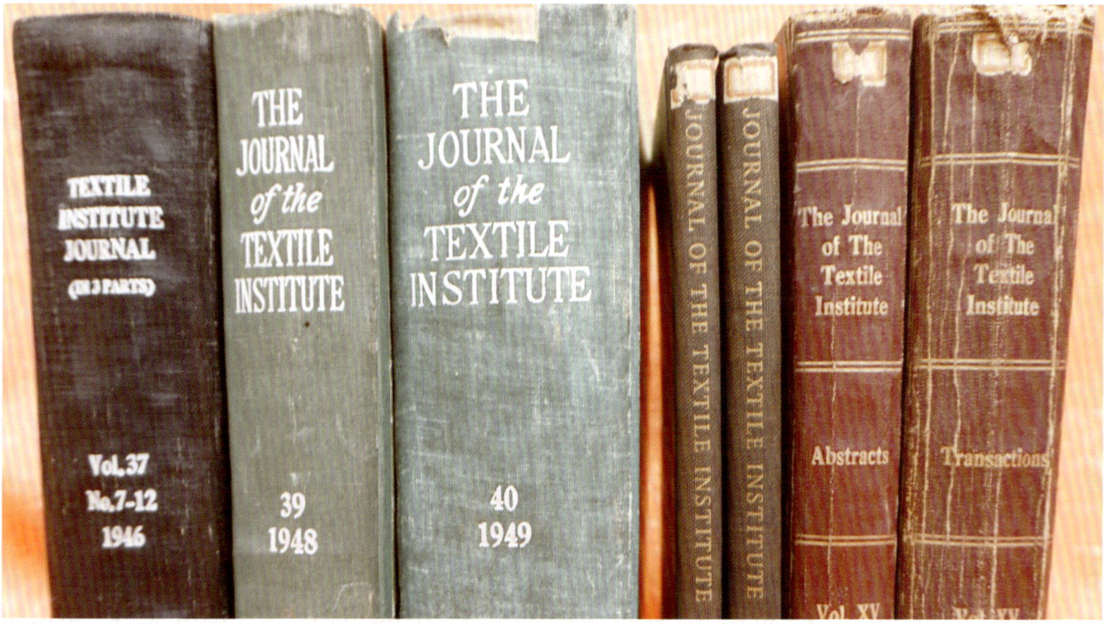

出版者：Textile Insitutte,Manchester

发行时间：创刊于 1910 年，收藏 1910-1949 年出版的刊物 75 本，按主题和文献类型出版

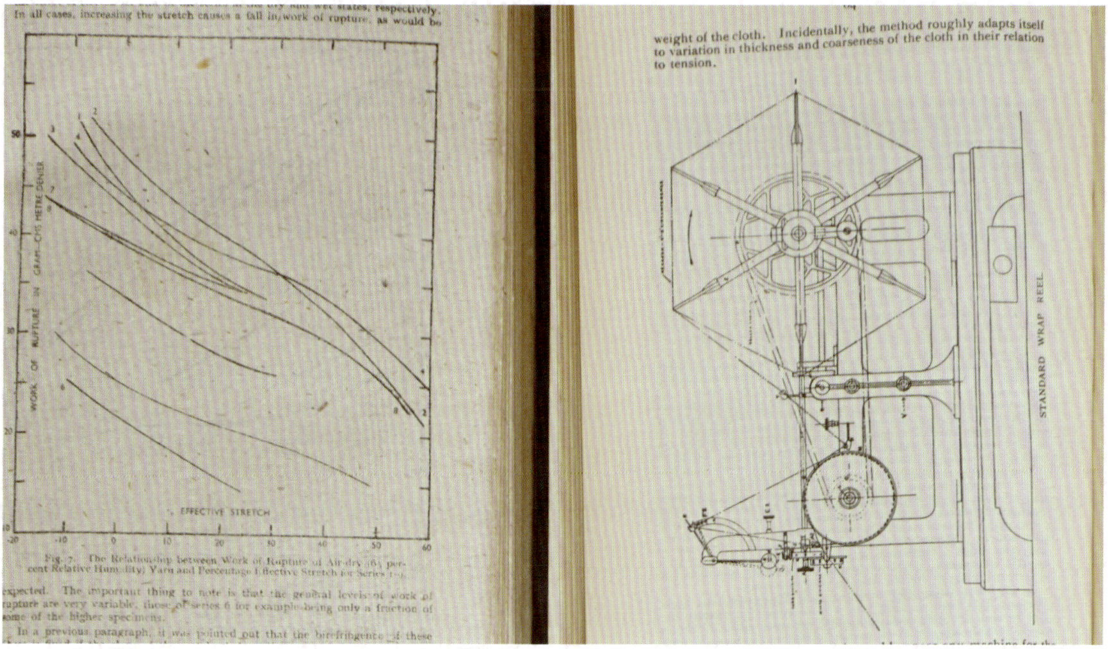

Melliand Textilberichte

出版者：Rodman Publishing Co.
发行时间：创刊于 1909 年，
收藏 1920-1929 年出版的刊物 10 本